D1795992

CONTRIBUTORS

John E. Allen

Sue Becklake

Robert Burton

Barry Cox

Jacqueline Dineen

Plantagenet Somerset Fry

Bill Gunston

Robin Kerrod

Kaye Orten

Peter Stephens

Aubrey Tulley

Tom Williamson

Thomas Wright

ARTISTS

Fred Anderson

Geoffrey Burns

Richard Eastland

Philip Emms

Dan Escott/John Sibbick

John Fraser

Elizabeth Graham-Yool

Richard Hook

Eric Jewell

Ben Manchipp

Angus McBride

Photo Credits
Boston Medical Library; Paul Brierly;
BBC Stills Library; J. Allan Cash;
Douglas Dickens, FRPS;
Glaxo Laboratories Ltd; Mansell Collection;
Microcolour Ltd (Gene Cox);
Pace Photography; Science Museum;
Tanzanian High Commission;
Transworld Feature Syndicate Inc;
Robert Updegraff; Wellcome Institute; Zefa.

Front cover: Tony Duffy/All-Sport.

CHIEF EDUCATIONAL ADVISER

Lynda Snowdon
Infant School Headteacher

TEACHER ADVISORY PANEL

Helen Craddock
Infant School Headteacher

John Enticknap
Author and Primary School Headteacher

Arthur Razzell
Lecturer in Child Development,
Author and Headteacher

EDITORIAL BOARD

Philip M. Clark   Executive Editor
Jan Burgess   Assistant Editor
Ethel Hurwicz   Picture Researcher

DESIGNERS

Faulkner/Marks

© Macmillan Publishers Limited, 1979
All rights reserved. No part of this
publication may be reproduced or transmitted
in any form or by any means, without permission

First published in 1979
Reprinted in 1981, 1982, 1983 by
Macmillan Children's Books
a division of Macmillan Publishers Limited
4 Little Essex Street, London WC2R 3LF
Associated companies throughout the world

ISBN 0 333 25270 5 (volume 1)
ISBN 0 333 19444 6 (complete set)

Printed in Hong Kong

You and Your Body

LOOK IT UP

Contents

This is Joe Grant. Joe lives with his Mum and Dad and his sister Anna. Joe's Dad has a mother and father too. They are Grandpa and Grandma Grant.

Joe's Mum often goes to see her mother and father. They are called Grandad and Granny Stone.

Joe Grant

YOU AND YOUR FAMILY

People sometimes talk about a 'family tree'. You can think of your own family as a kind of tree. The trunk represents your parents. The roots are your grandparents. The branches are you and your brothers and sisters. This picture shows the family tree of the Grant family.

Mr Grant

Grandpa and Grandma Grant

Anna Grant

This is Anna Grant. Anna has one brother, Joe. Anna is the youngest in the family. She is seven. Grandpa Grant is the oldest. He is 76. You can see in the picture that Anna and Joe have two parents and four grandparents. But they have lots of other relations as well.

Mrs Grant

Grandad and Granny Stone

There are three levels in a tree. They are the roots, the trunk and the branches. There are three levels in the Grant family. Each level in a family is called a generation.

Grandpa and Grandma Grant and Grandad and Granny Stone are one generation. Mum and Dad Grant are another generation. The third generation is Joe and Anna Grant. They are the youngest generation.

Relations

Here are Joe and Anna with more of their relations. There are really two family trees here. Can you see where they join?

Mum and Dad Grant are friendly with Uncle Bob and Auntie Sue. Mum Grant only has one brother. He is Joe and Anna's Uncle Bob. Your parents' brothers and sisters are your aunts and uncles.

Grandpa and Grandma Grant only have one son. But they have two grandchildren, Joe and Anna.

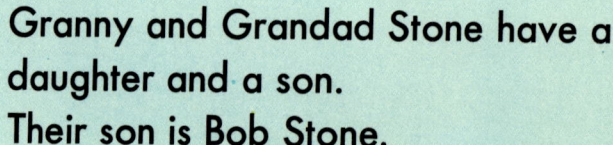

Granny and Grandad Stone have a daughter and a son. Their son is Bob Stone.

The children of your aunts and uncles are called your cousins. Matthew and Lucy Stone are Joe and Anna's cousins.

Here are Uncle Bob and Auntie Sue Stone. They are in Mum and Dad Grant's generation. Joe Grant is Uncle Bob and Auntie Sue's nephew. Anna Grant is their niece.

Auntie Sue's Mum and Dad live nearby. Joe and Anna call them Aunt Kate and Uncle Frank. Can you see who else is part of their generation? Who are their grandchildren?

Kinds of families

In some parts of the world a man may have more than one wife. The top picture shows a chief in Southern Africa with all his wives.

The big picture shows a 'long house' in Sarawak, south-east Asia. 160 families live in it as one group.

The small picture shows a very common kind of family – two parents and their children.

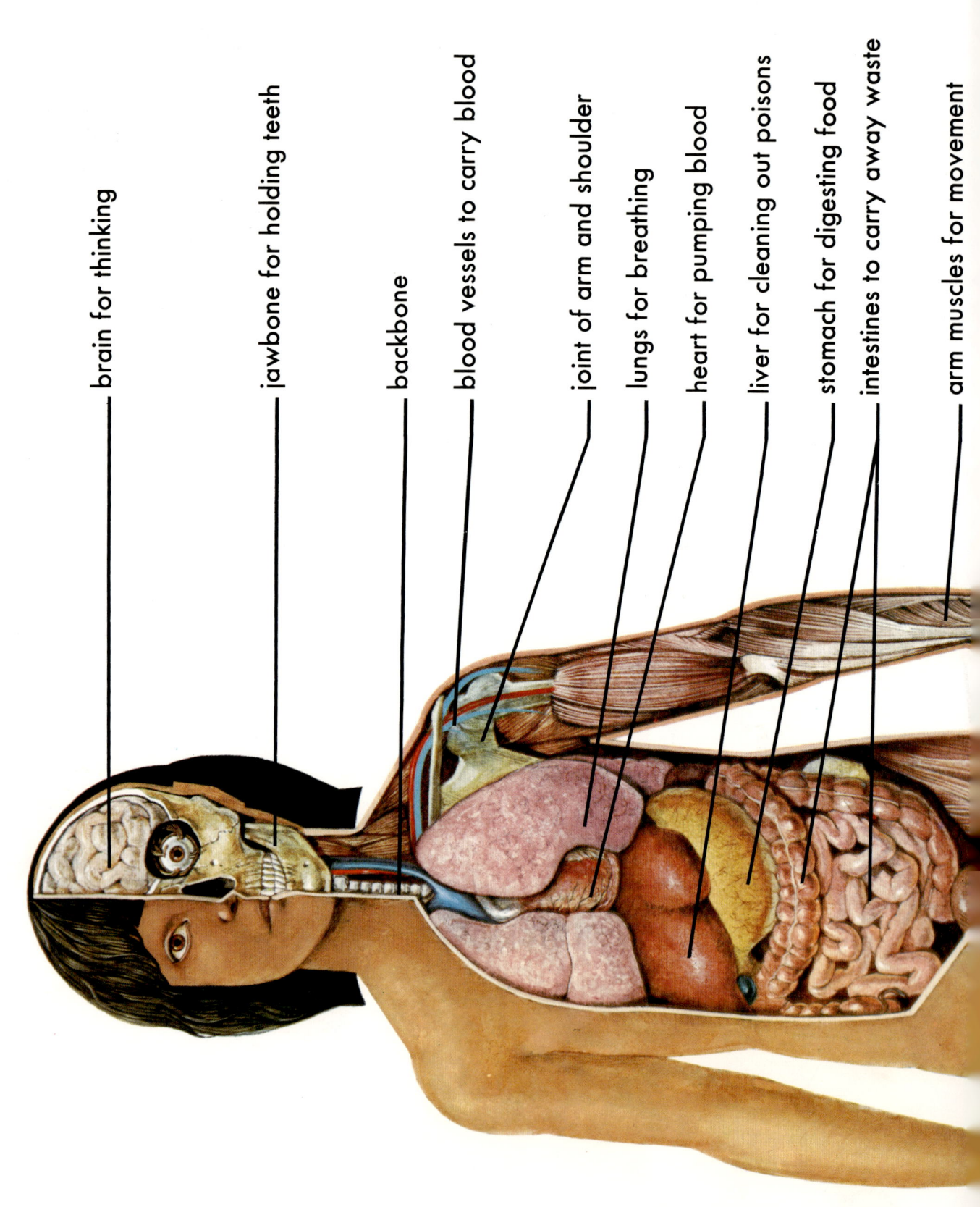

brain for thinking

jawbone for holding teeth

backbone

blood vessels to carry blood

joint of arm and shoulder

lungs for breathing

heart for pumping blood

liver for cleaning out poisons

stomach for digesting food

intestines to carry away waste

arm muscles for movement

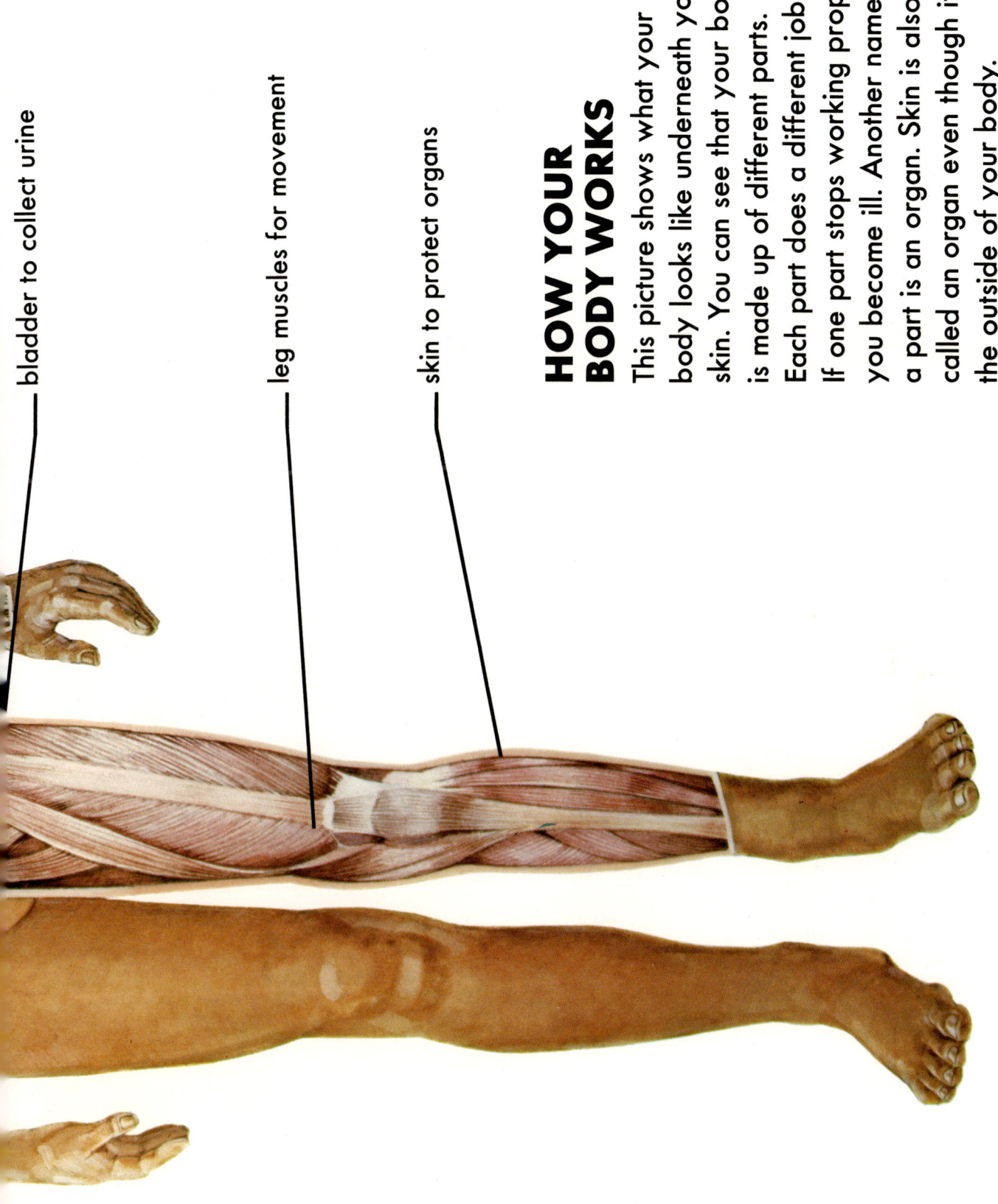

bladder to collect urine

leg muscles for movement

skin to protect organs

HOW YOUR BODY WORKS

This picture shows what your body looks like underneath your skin. You can see that your body is made up of different parts. Each part does a different job. If one part stops working properly, you become ill. Another name for a part is an organ. Skin is also called an organ even though it is the outside of your body.

Skin and hair

Your skin does lots of important jobs. It protects the organs of your body from dirt and germs. It also helps to keep your body at the same temperature. When you get hot you perspire through your skin. This water evaporates away and makes you cooler.

Everyone has different fingerprints. Try inking the tips of your fingers on an ink pad. Then press your fingers onto a piece of paper. Your fingerprints will show up clearly.

Different races of people have different coloured skin.
This girl belongs to a group that is sometimes called 'yellow-skinned'. Her family came from south-east Asia.

Special substances called pigments give skin its colour. How dark your skin is depends on how much pigment it contains. This girl has a dark skin. Her skin has a lot of pigment in it.

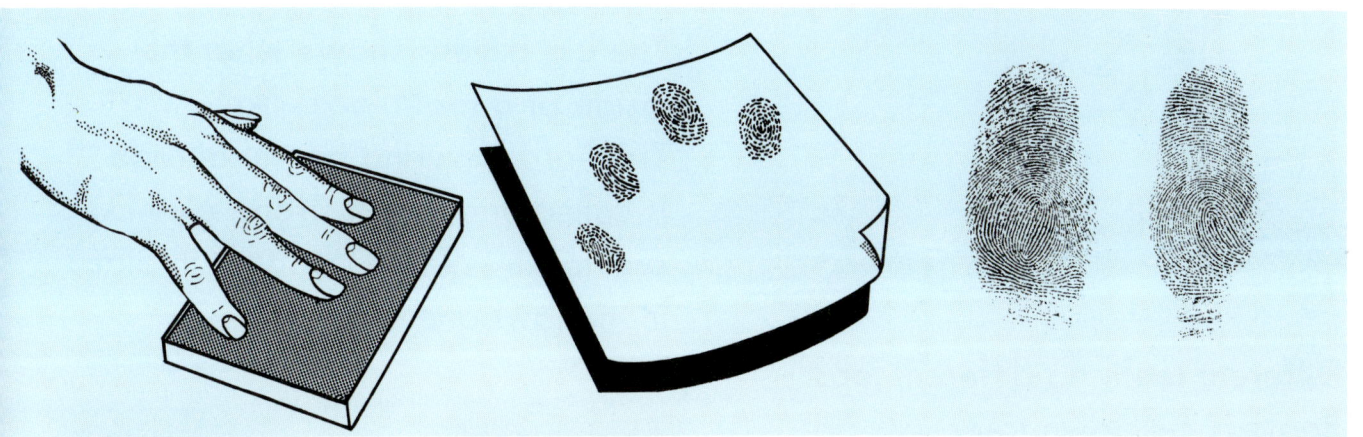

Everybody has some colour in their skin. This girl's skin only has a small amount of pigment in it. Today people with different coloured skins have moved all over the world.

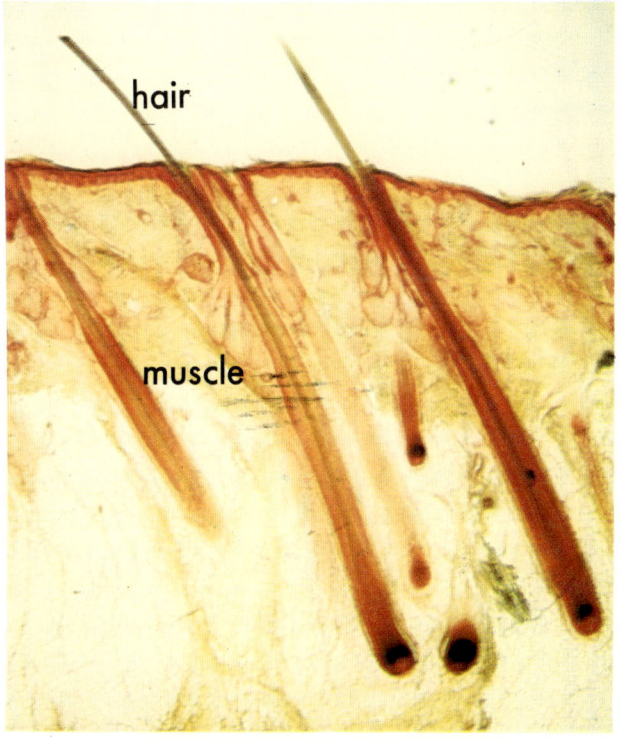

hair

muscle

This picture shows the parts just under the skin. Everything is shown much larger than it really is. Hairs grow through the skin almost all over the body. Most of them are so fine you can hardly see them. You get 'goose pimples' when tiny muscles at the roots of your hairs make them stand up.

Different teeth do different jobs. Beavers cut down trees with flat front teeth called incisors.

Cows have square back teeth called molars for chewing.

Cats have pointed teeth called canines for tearing up meat.

Teeth

The big picture shows what the inside of a tooth looks like.
The hard covering on the outside is called enamel. A strong glue-like substance holds each tooth in place in the jawbone.

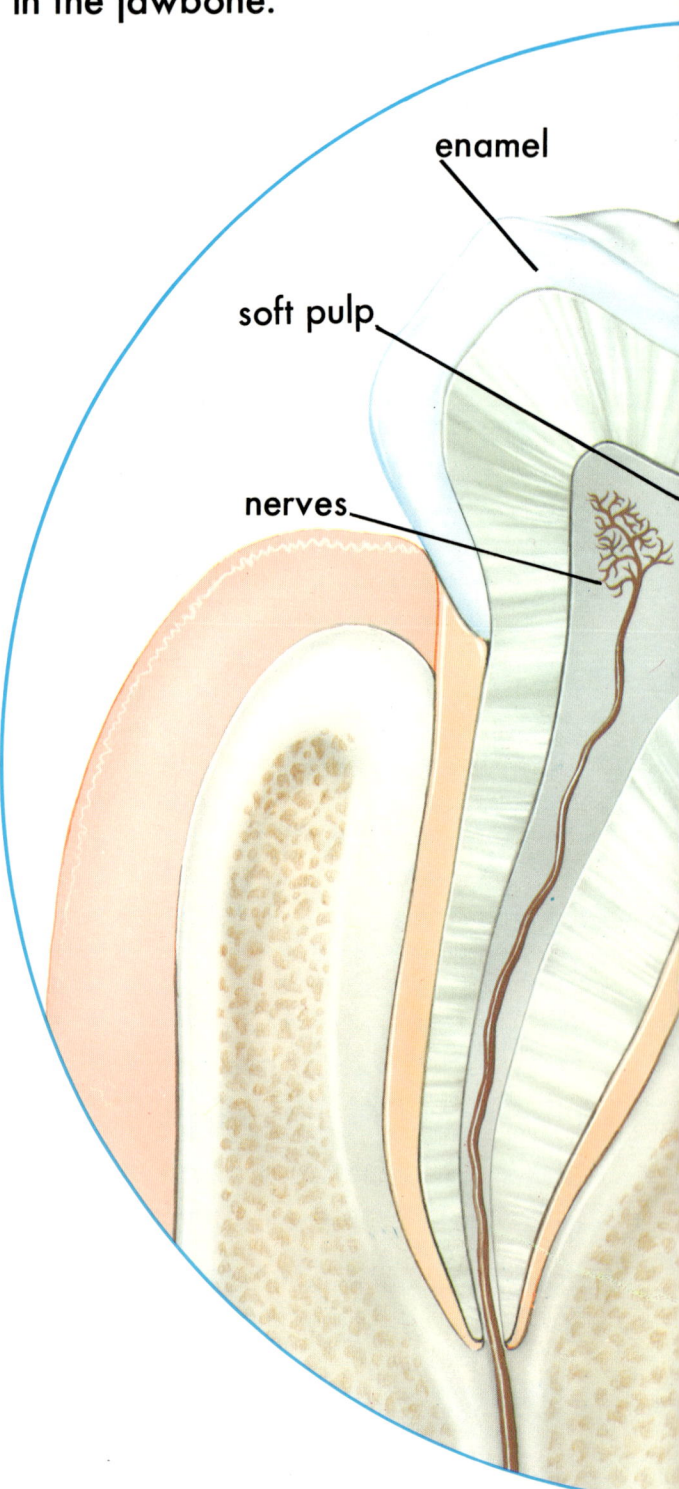

enamel

soft pulp

nerves

Underneath the enamel is the dentine, which is like bone. In the middle of the tooth is soft pulp. Inside the pulp are the blood vessels and nerves.

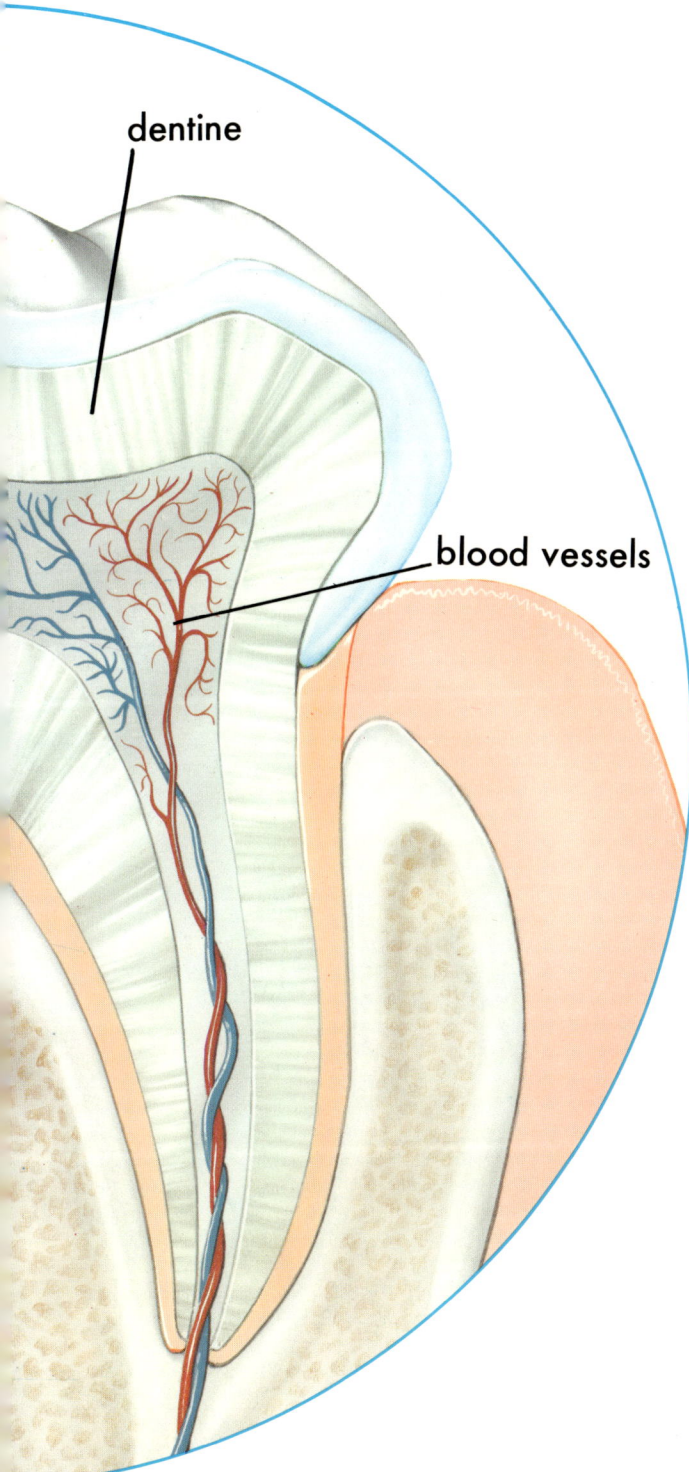

dentine

blood vessels

You have three kinds of teeth: incisors, molars and canines. This is because you eat a variety of different food.

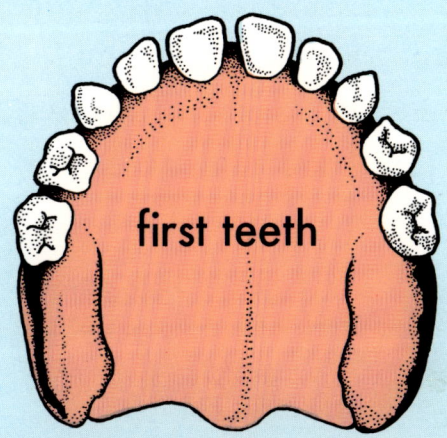

first teeth

Your first teeth are sometimes called milk teeth. When you are about seven, your first teeth come out one by one.

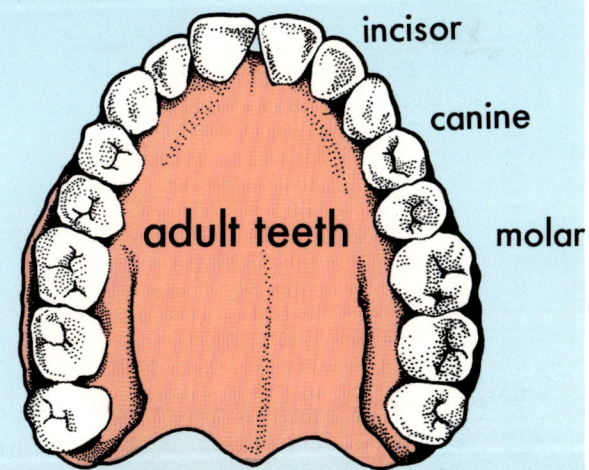

incisor

canine

adult teeth

molar

Your first teeth are replaced by larger adult teeth. There are 32 adult teeth altogether.

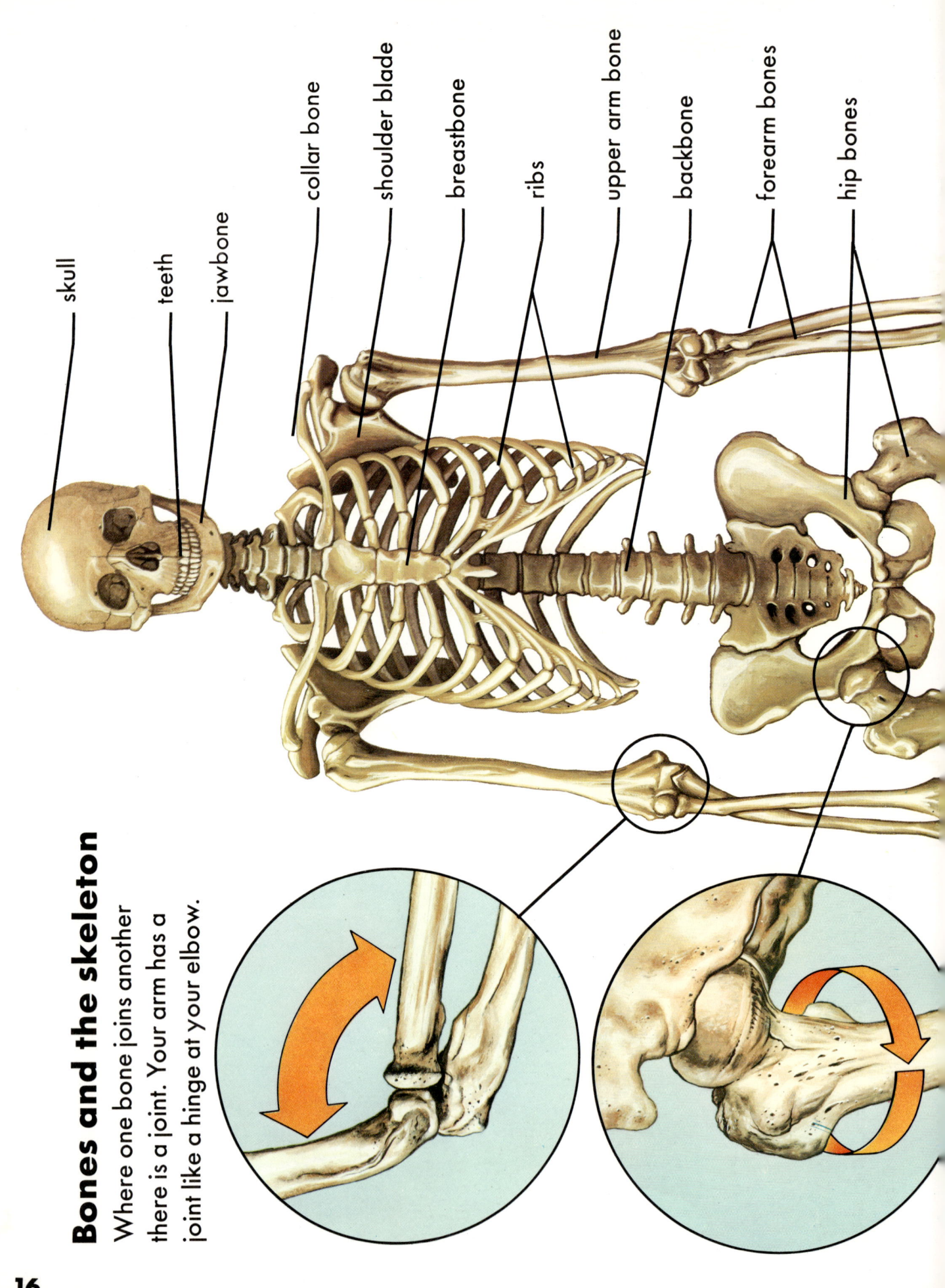

skull

teeth

jawbone

collar bone

shoulder blade

breastbone

ribs

upper arm bone

backbone

forearm bones

hip bones

Bones and the skeleton

Where one bone joins another there is a joint. Your arm has a joint like a hinge at your elbow.

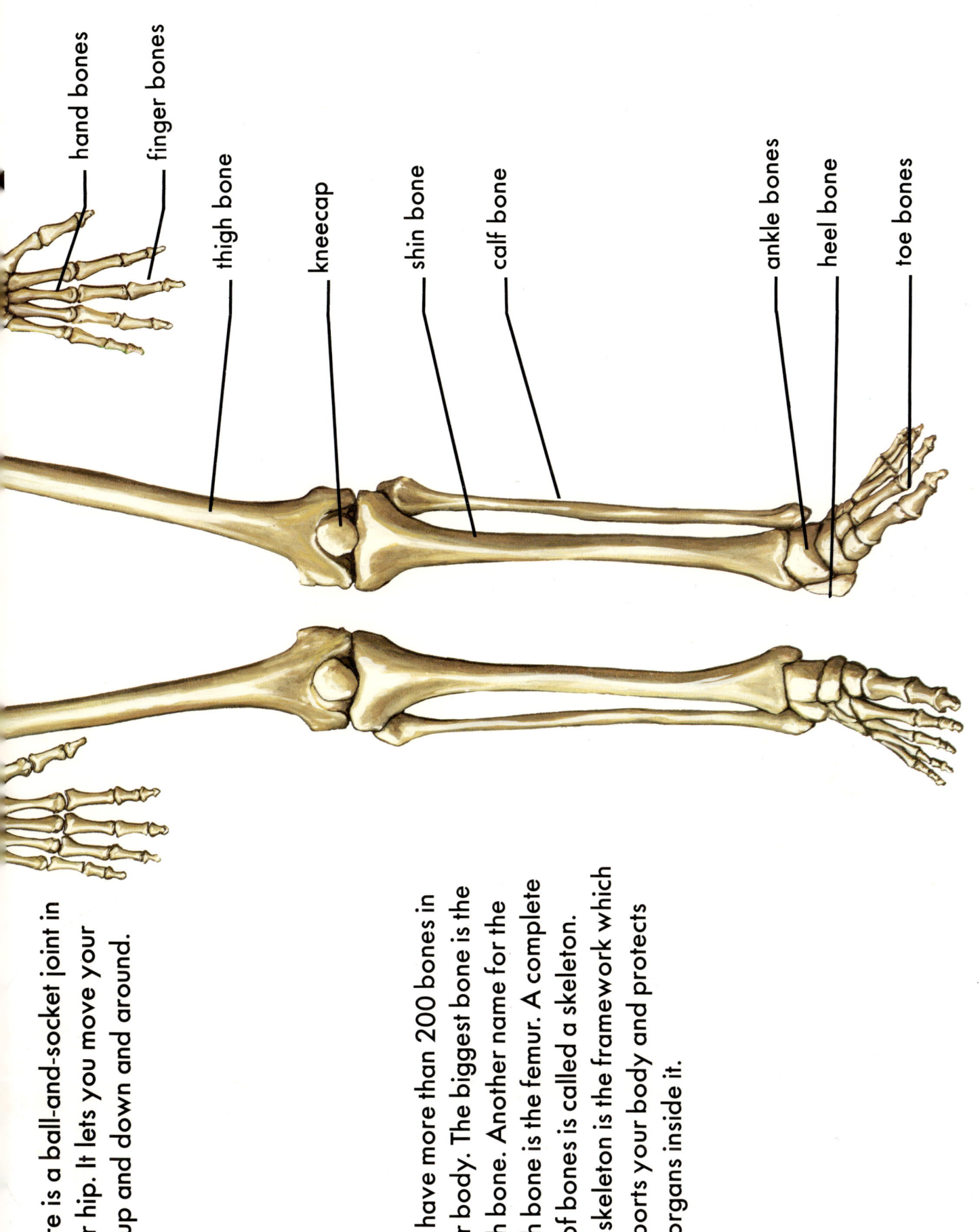

hand bones

finger bones

thigh bone

kneecap

shin bone

calf bone

ankle bones

heel bone

toe bones

There is a ball-and-socket joint in your hip. It lets you move your leg up and down and around.

You have more than 200 bones in your body. The biggest bone is the thigh bone. Another name for the thigh bone is the femur. A complete set of bones is called a skeleton. The skeleton is the framework which supports your body and protects the organs inside it.

17

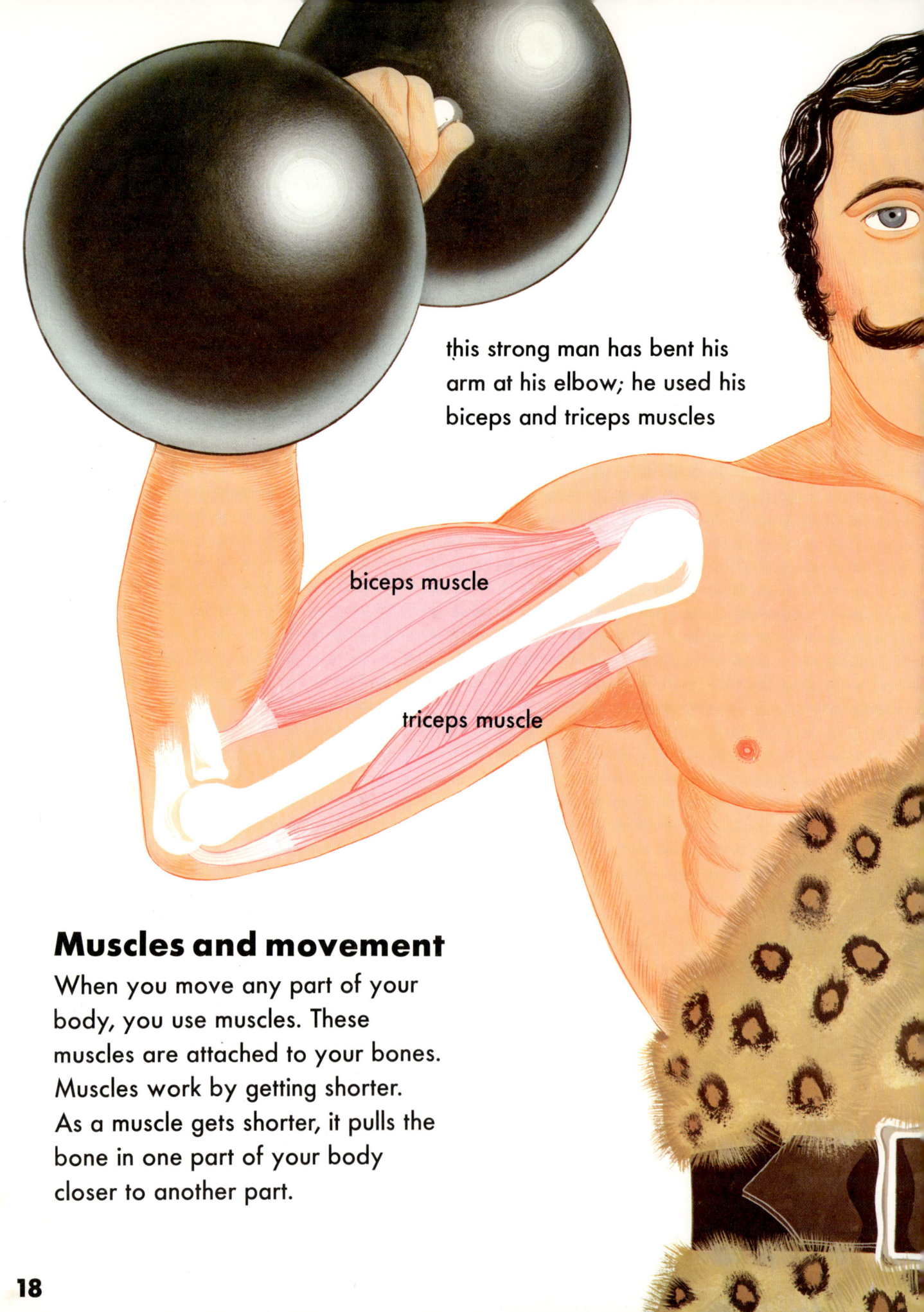

this strong man has bent his arm at his elbow; he used his biceps and triceps muscles

biceps muscle

triceps muscle

Muscles and movement

When you move any part of your body, you use muscles. These muscles are attached to your bones. Muscles work by getting shorter. As a muscle gets shorter, it pulls the bone in one part of your body closer to another part.

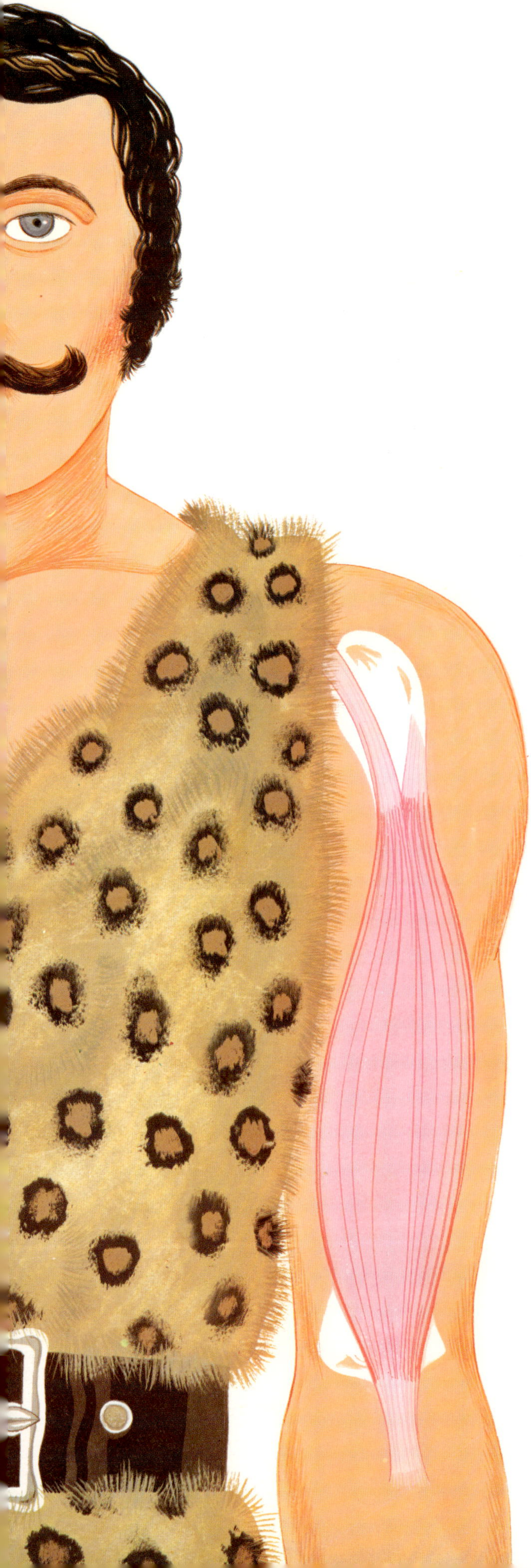

Muscles in your legs help you to walk upstairs. Muscles in your cheeks work your jaw so that you can open your mouth when you want to eat.

Blood

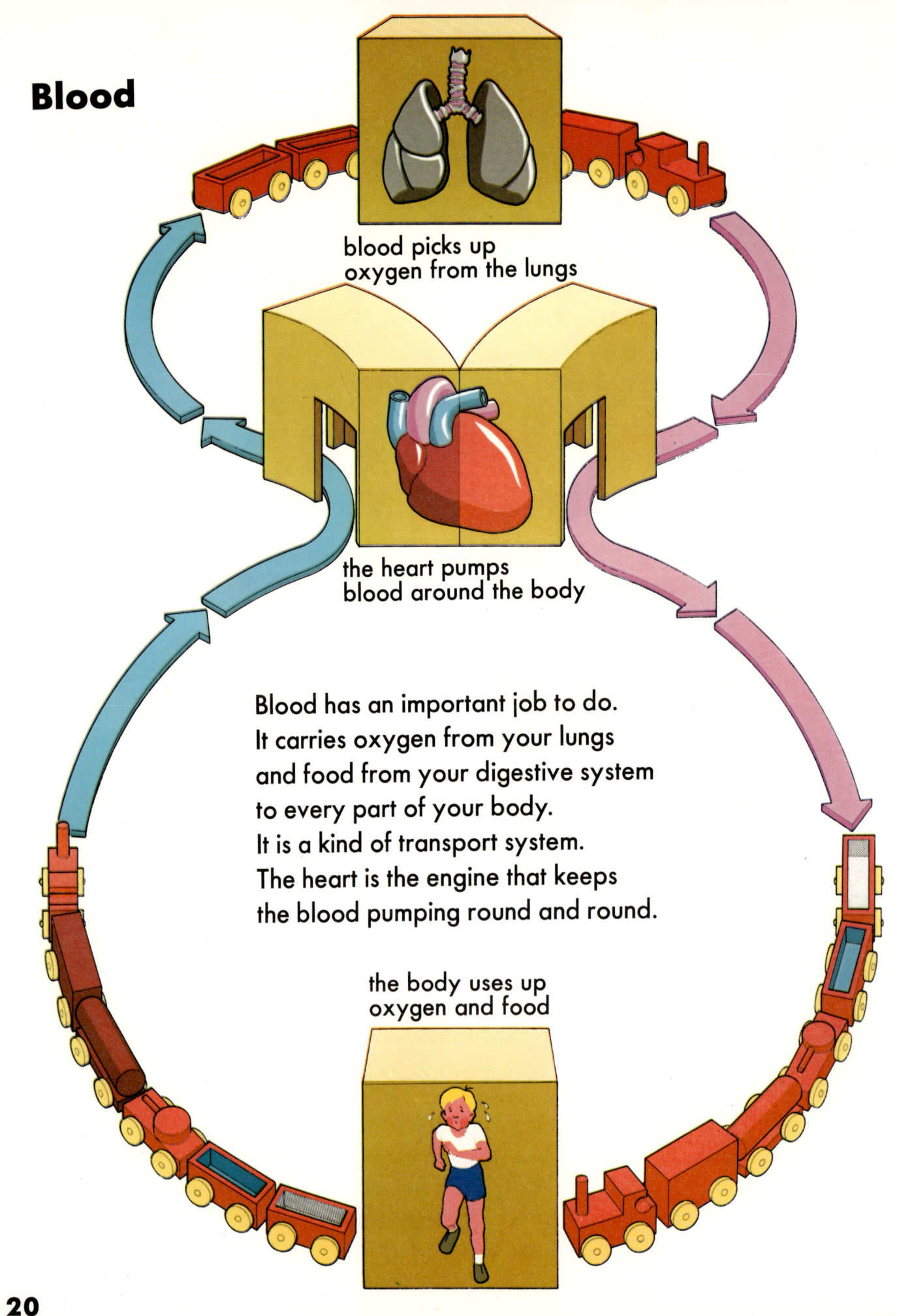

blood picks up
oxygen from the lungs

the heart pumps
blood around the body

Blood has an important job to do.
It carries oxygen from your lungs
and food from your digestive system
to every part of your body.
It is a kind of transport system.
The heart is the engine that keeps
the blood pumping round and round.

the body uses up
oxygen and food

Blood travels in thin tubes called blood vessels. The vessels are all joined up into a complicated network. It carries blood all over your body.

The bigger you are, the more blood your body contains. A baby only has enough blood to fill about 1½ litre bottles. A child has enough blood to fill about 3 litre bottles. A grown-up's blood would fill about 5 litre bottles.

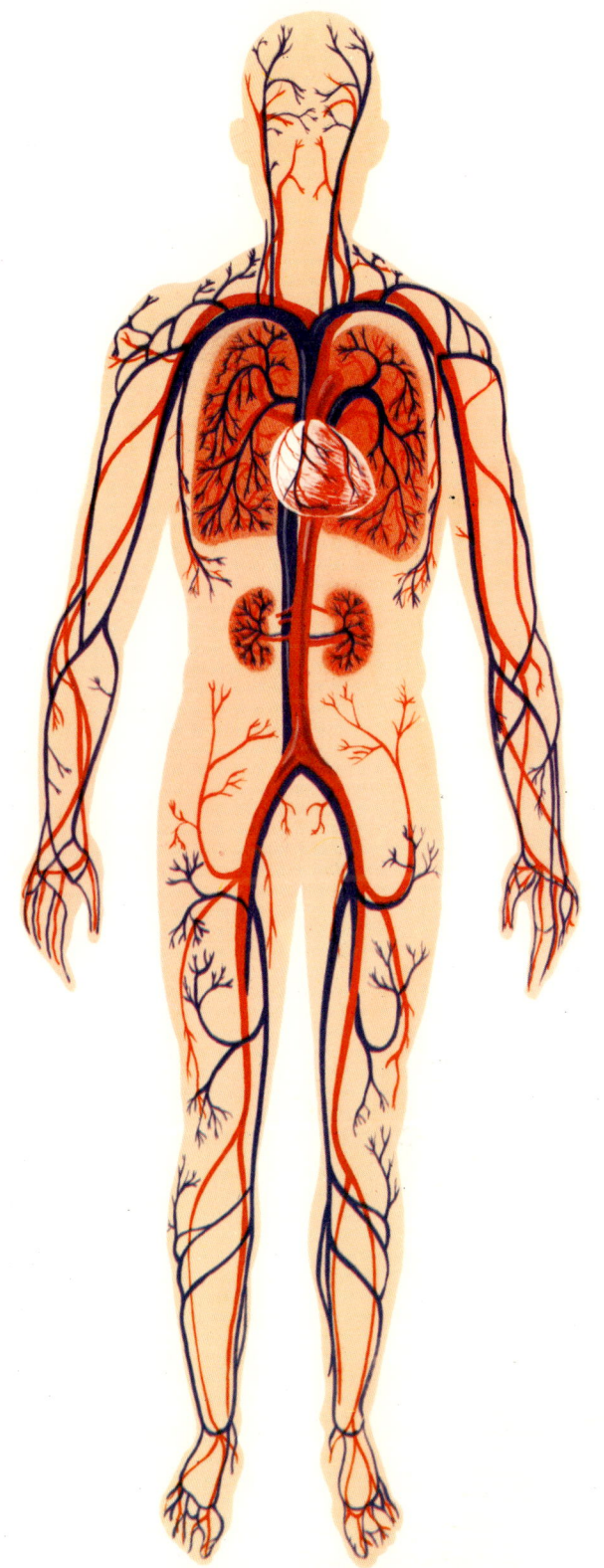

The red lines show blood vessels full of oxygen going away from the heart and lungs. The blue lines show blood coming back again to the heart and lungs.

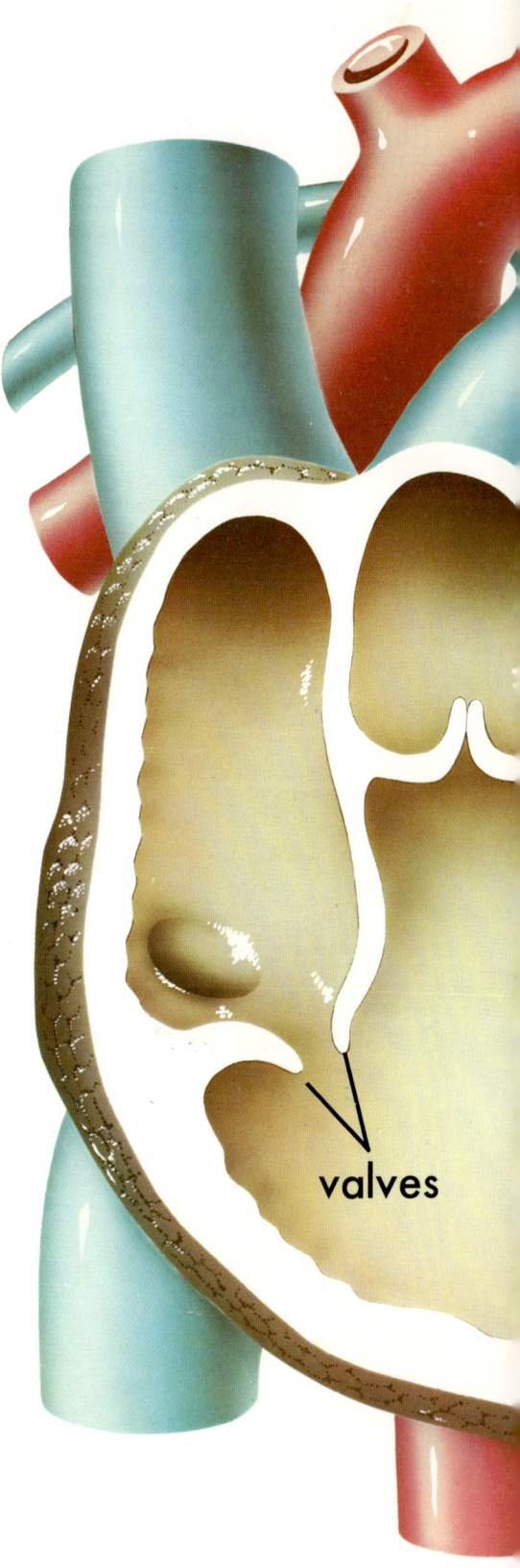

valves

The heart

Your heart is a kind of pump.
It pumps blood out to all parts of
your body. Inside the heart are
spaces called chambers.
The chambers fill with blood which
is ready to be pumped round your
body again. The chambers are
separated by valves. Valves are
rather like doors. They open and
close to let blood in and out of
the heart.

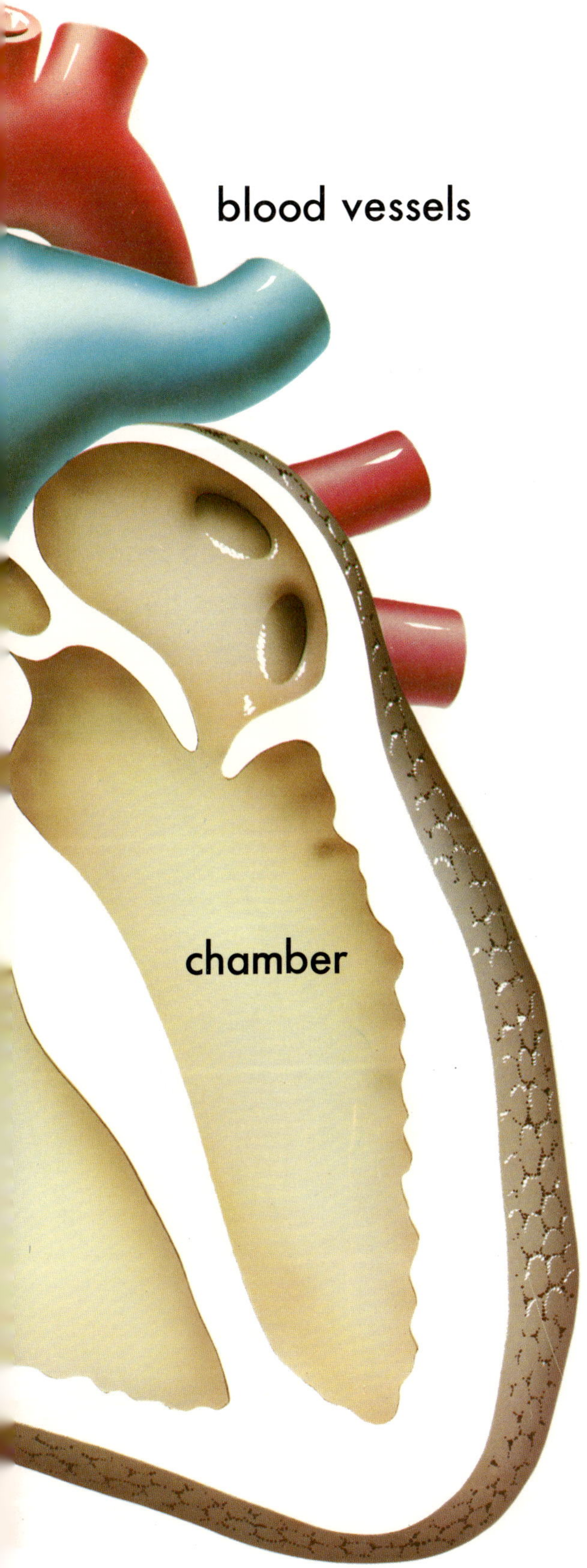

blood vessels

chamber

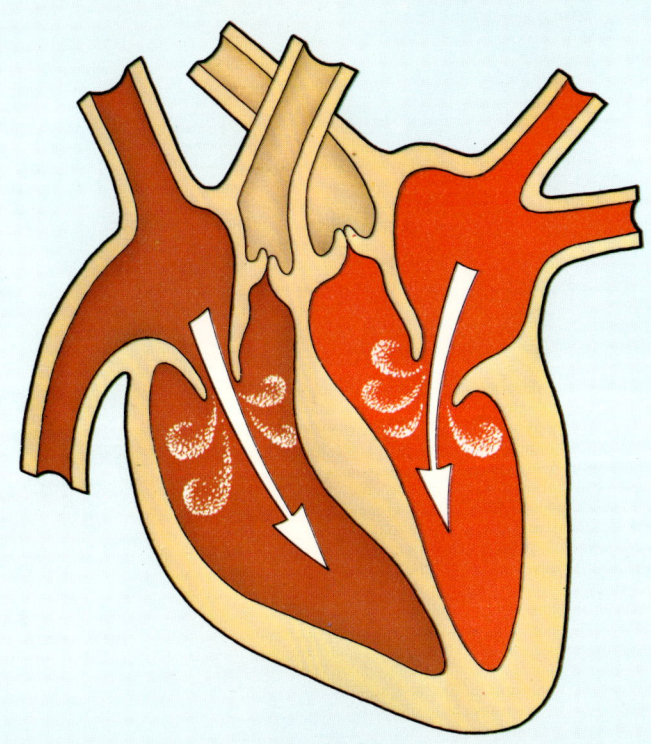

Blood is now rushing into the heart. The valves which let blood into the heart are open.

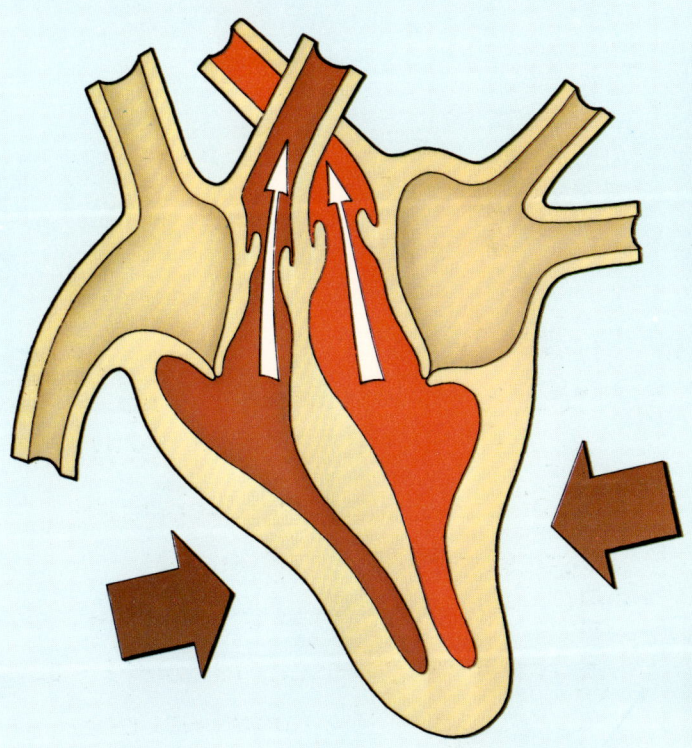

Blood is now being squeezed out of the heart. This is called a heart-beat.

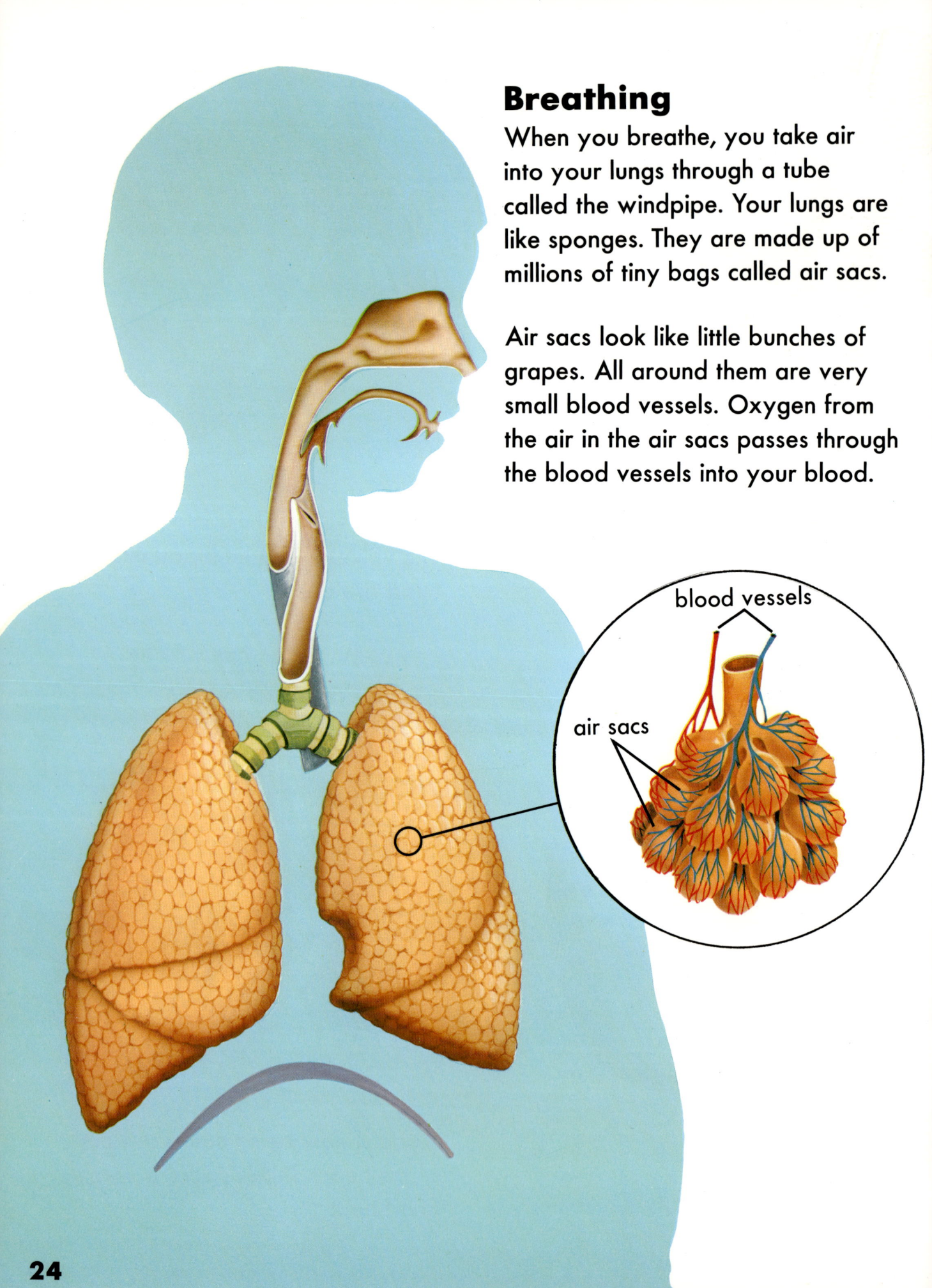

Breathing

When you breathe, you take air into your lungs through a tube called the windpipe. Your lungs are like sponges. They are made up of millions of tiny bags called air sacs.

Air sacs look like little bunches of grapes. All around them are very small blood vessels. Oxygen from the air in the air sacs passes through the blood vessels into your blood.

blood vessels

air sacs

you can blow out about two litres of air with one big blow

Your lungs are protected by bones called ribs. The ribs make a kind of cage round your lungs called the ribcage. When you breathe in your lungs fill up with air. They get bigger. Your ribcage also has to get bigger to make room for your lungs.

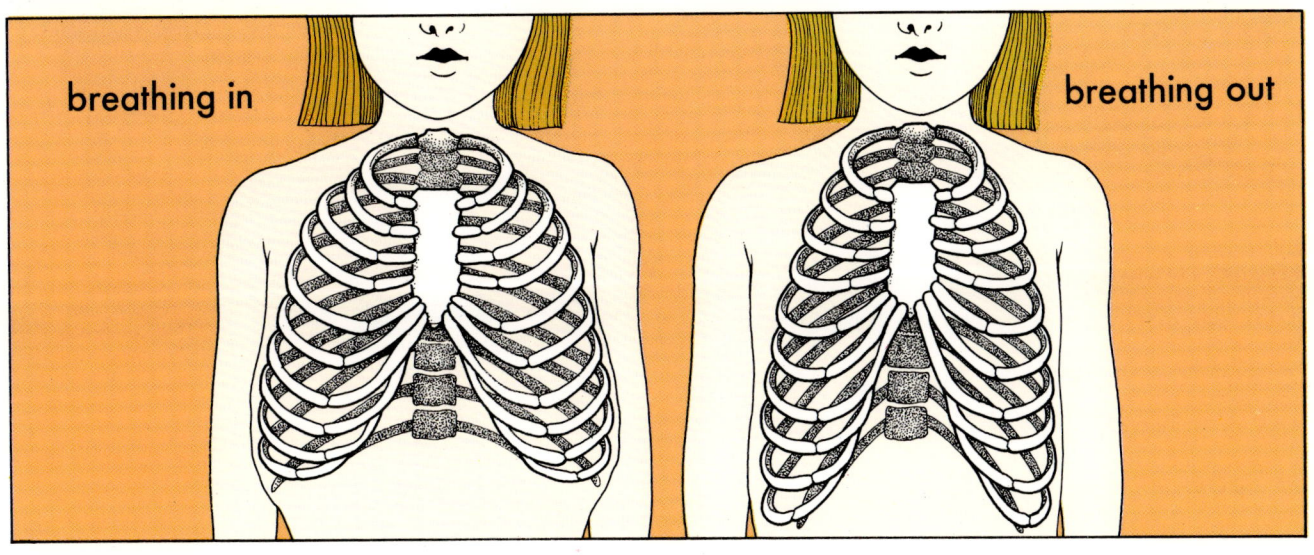

breathing in

breathing out

Why you need food

Feeling hungry is a sign that your body needs food. Some foods, like these, contain lots of protein. They help you grow and keep you fit and strong.

You also need food to give you energy. Foods which contain starch and sugar give you energy. You use up a lot of energy when you run around and play games.

These foods contain fats. Fat keeps you warm, but it is not a good idea to eat too much fat. Healthy people eat a mixture of all three kinds of food.

Your body also needs substances
called vitamins and minerals to
keep healthy. All the different foods
in this picture contain lots of
vitamins and minerals as well as
protein, starch and fat.

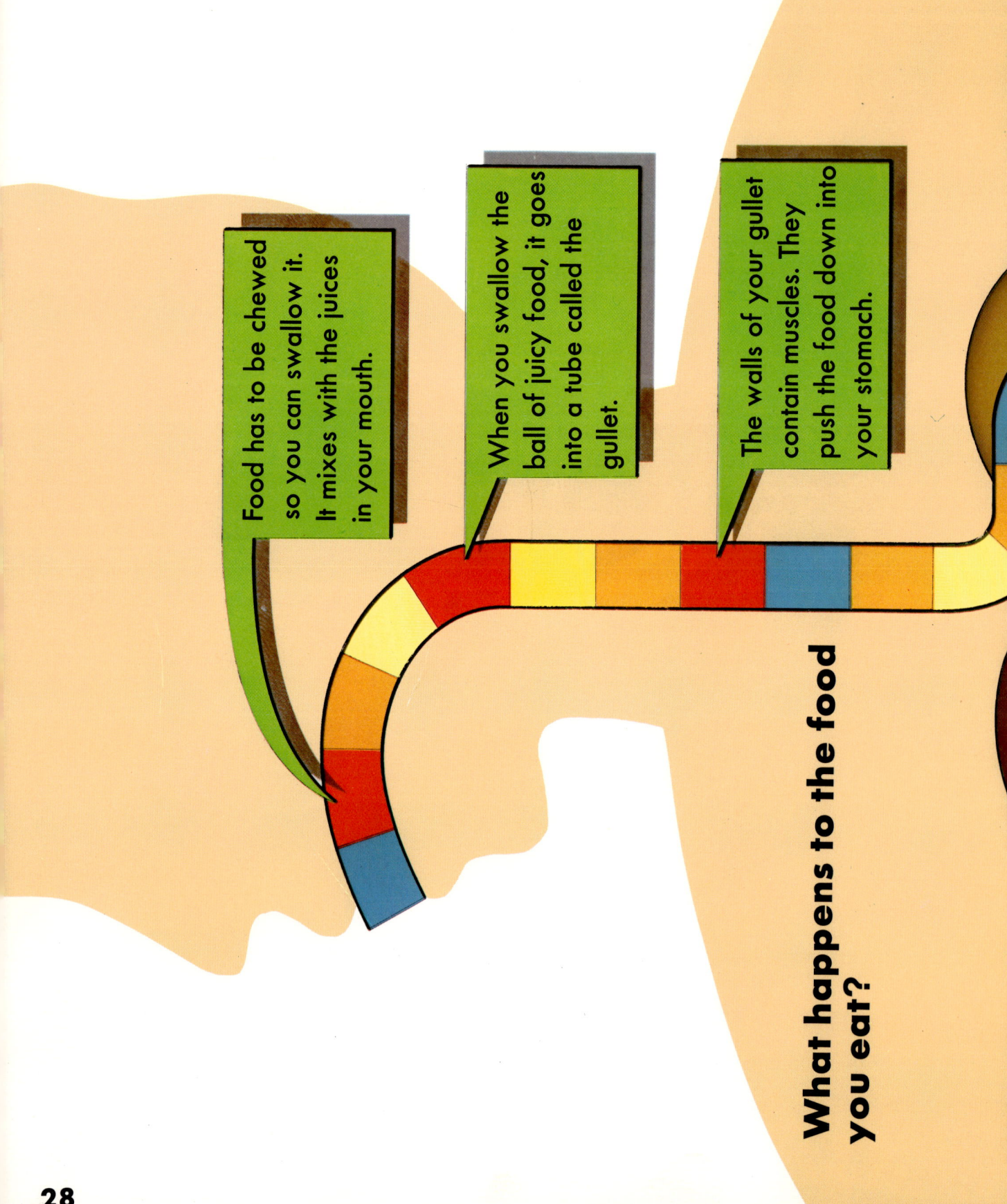

Food has to be chewed so you can swallow it. It mixes with the juices in your mouth.

When you swallow the ball of juicy food, it goes into a tube called the gullet.

The walls of your gullet contain muscles. They push the food down into your stomach.

What happens to the food you eat?

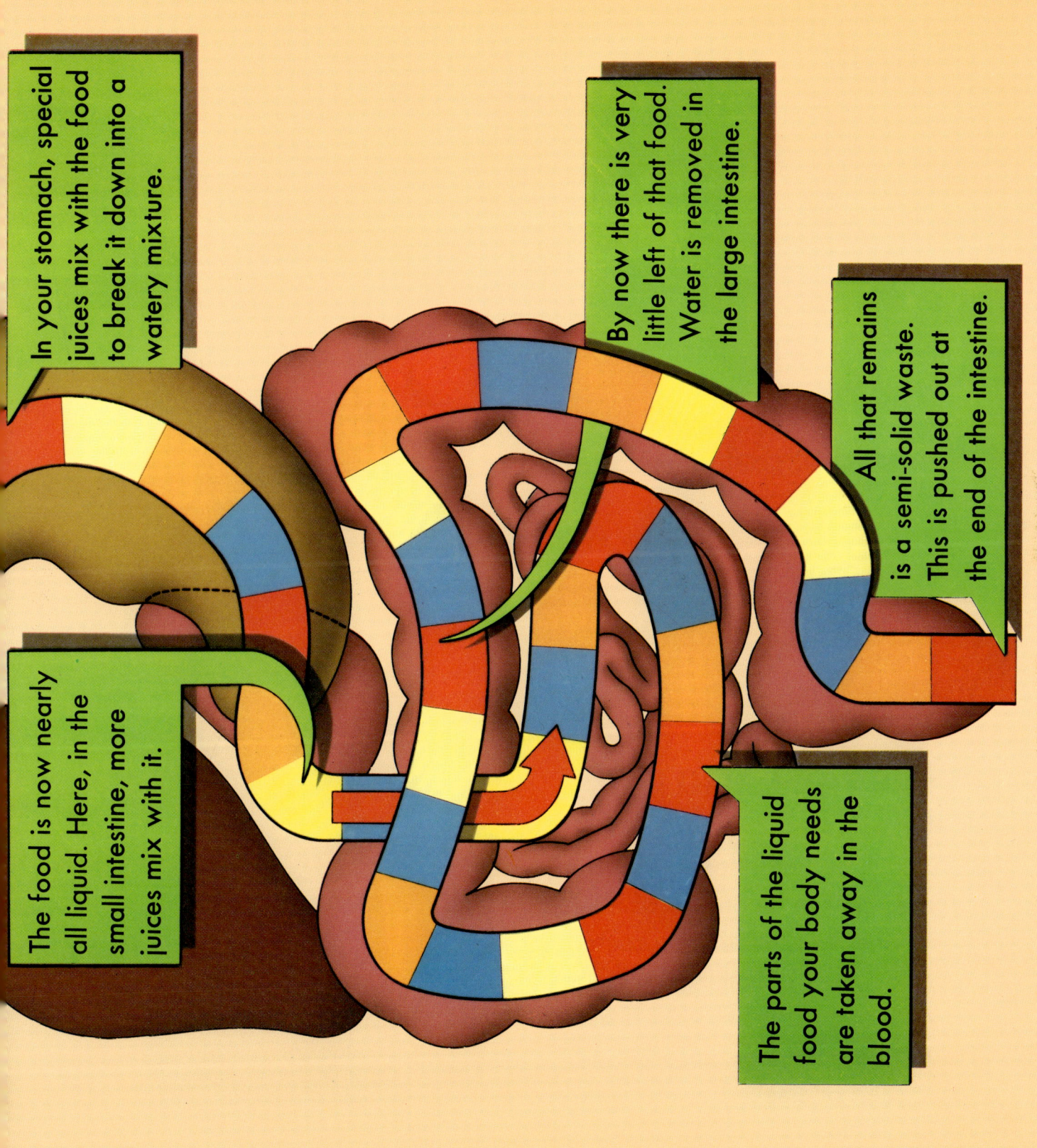

In your stomach, special juices mix with the food to break it down into a watery mixture.

By now there is very little left of that food. Water is removed in the large intestine.

All that remains is a semi-solid waste. This is pushed out at the end of the intestine.

The food is now nearly all liquid. Here, in the small intestine, more juices mix with it.

The parts of the liquid food your body needs are taken away in the blood.

THE BRAIN AND THE SENSES

You have nerves all over your body. Nerves act like a network of telephone lines. When you see or touch or smell something, messages travel along nerves to your brain. Your brain then tells you what you have seen or smelled or touched. Other nerves control muscles so that you can sit, stand, walk, run, skip and jump.

This boy likes ice-cream. When he looks at the ice-cream on the table, a message travels from his eye along a nerve to his brain, and he recognizes the ice-cream.

When he decides to eat the ice-cream, an order from the boy's brain travels along another nerve to his arm muscles. His brain tells his arm to pick up the ice-cream and lift it to his mouth.

Each part of the brain has its own job. Parts at the front and sides control movement.

A special area on the left-hand side of the brain controls speaking and singing.

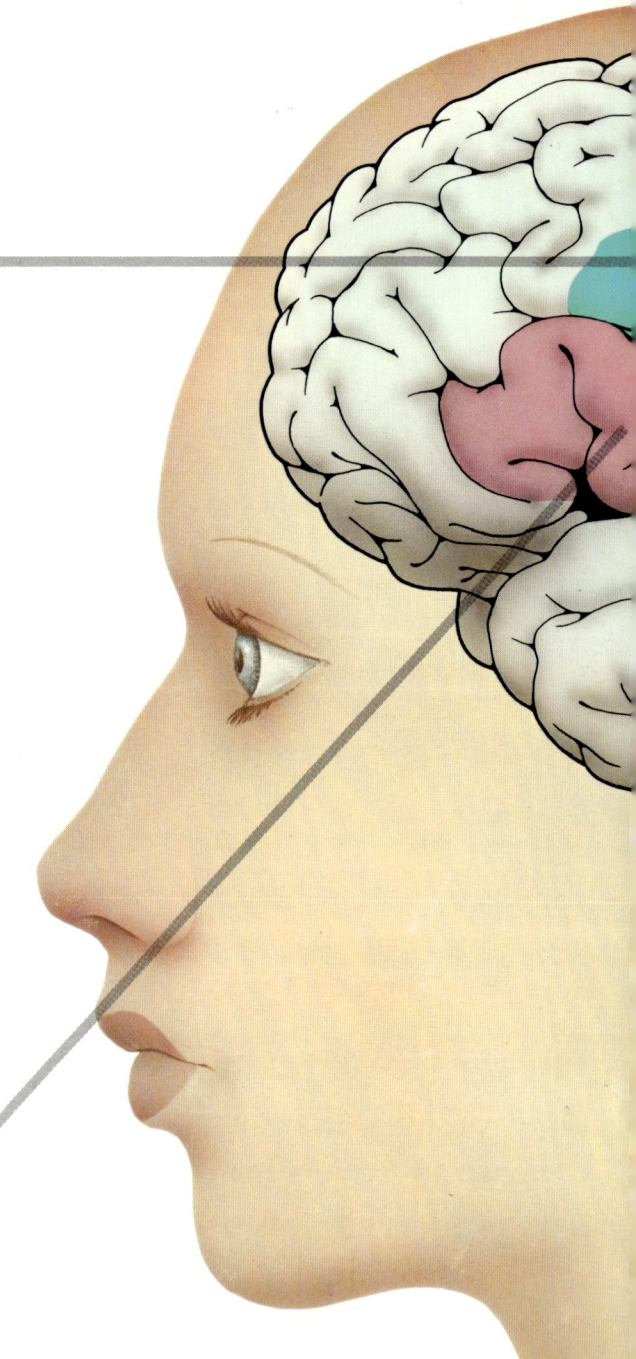

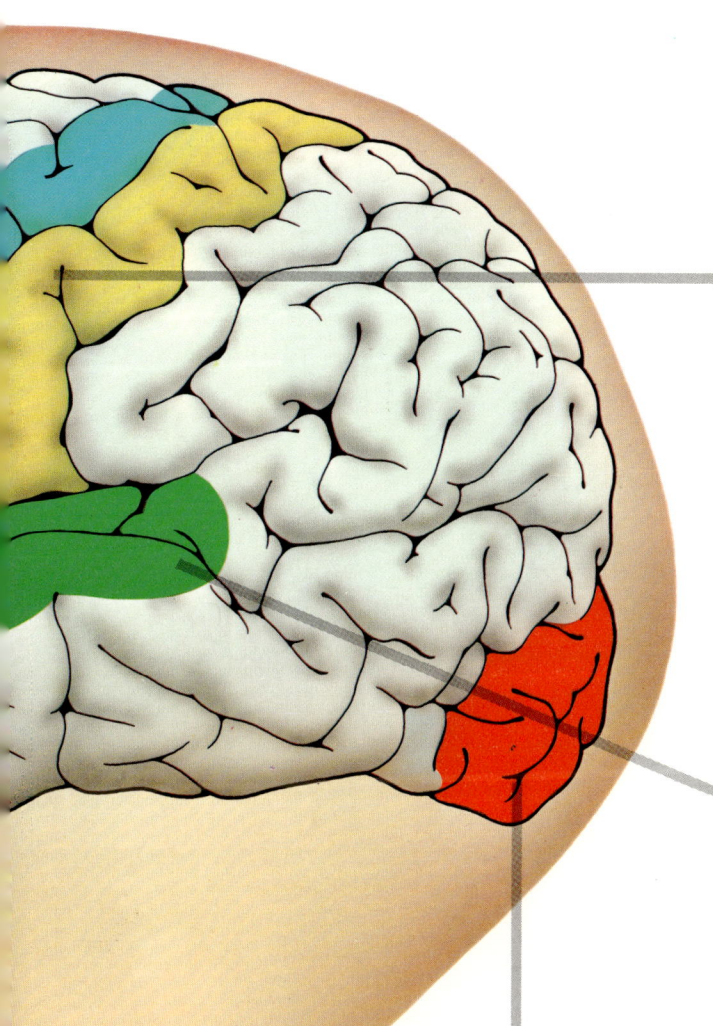

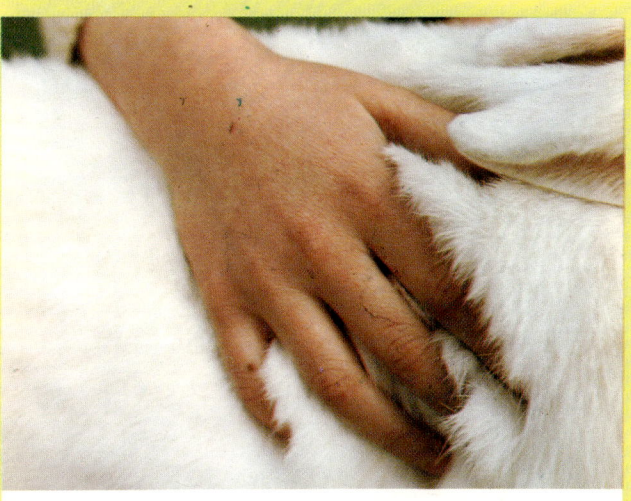

The sense of touch depends on another area of the brain. It tells you what things feel like.

The brain

Your brain is the control box of your body. Your brain is always working. It controls everything you do. It sends out orders and receives messages along nerves that go out to every part of your body.

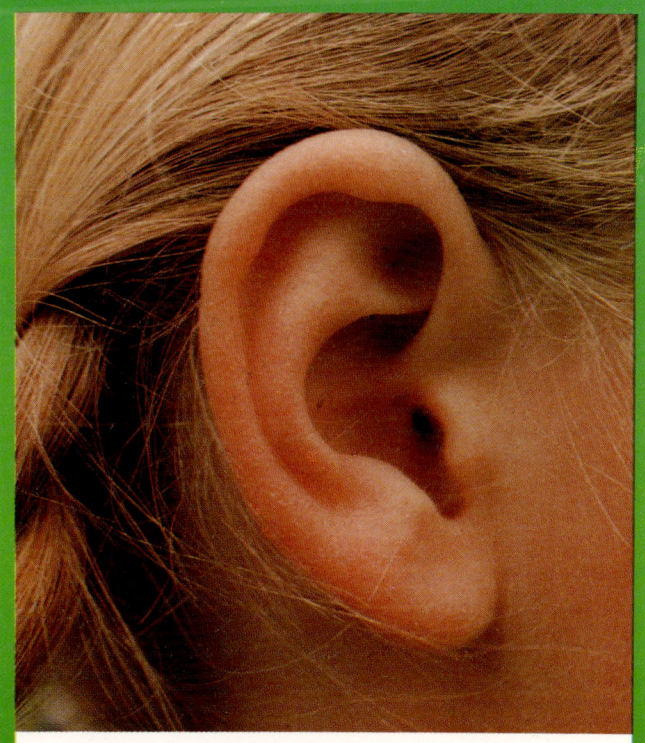

The part of your brain that controls hearing is below the area that controls touch.

Seeing

Your eyes are rather like round balls. When you look at someone's eyes, you only see part of the eyeball. The eyeball fits into a part of the skull called a socket.

You see things because of light coming into your eyes. The big picture shows how you see the clown. Light bounces off the clown into your eye. Your eye then sends a nerve message to your brain. The picture at the back of your eye is upside down but your brain makes you see it the right way up.

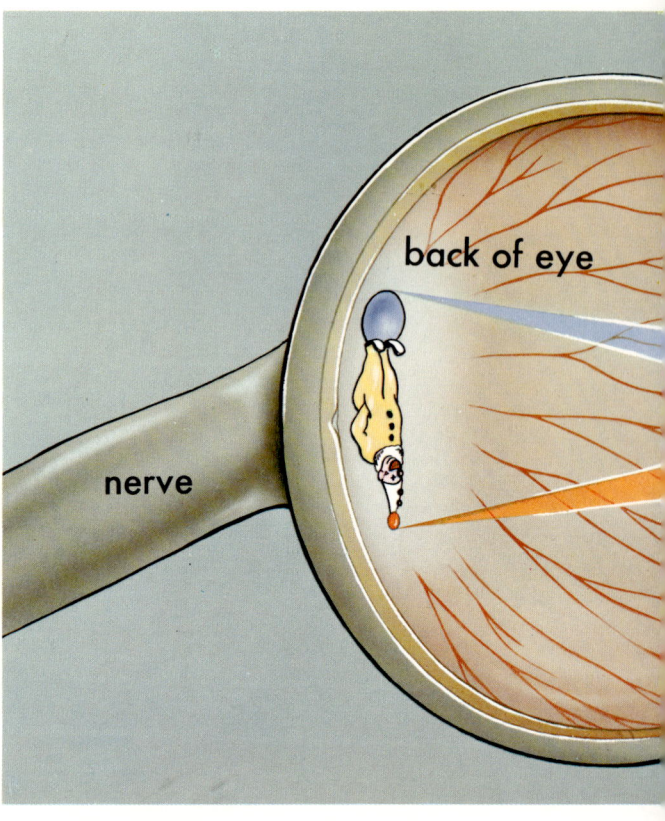

back of eye

nerve

If you look hard at something, things around it seem blurred. This is because you can only focus on one distance at a time.

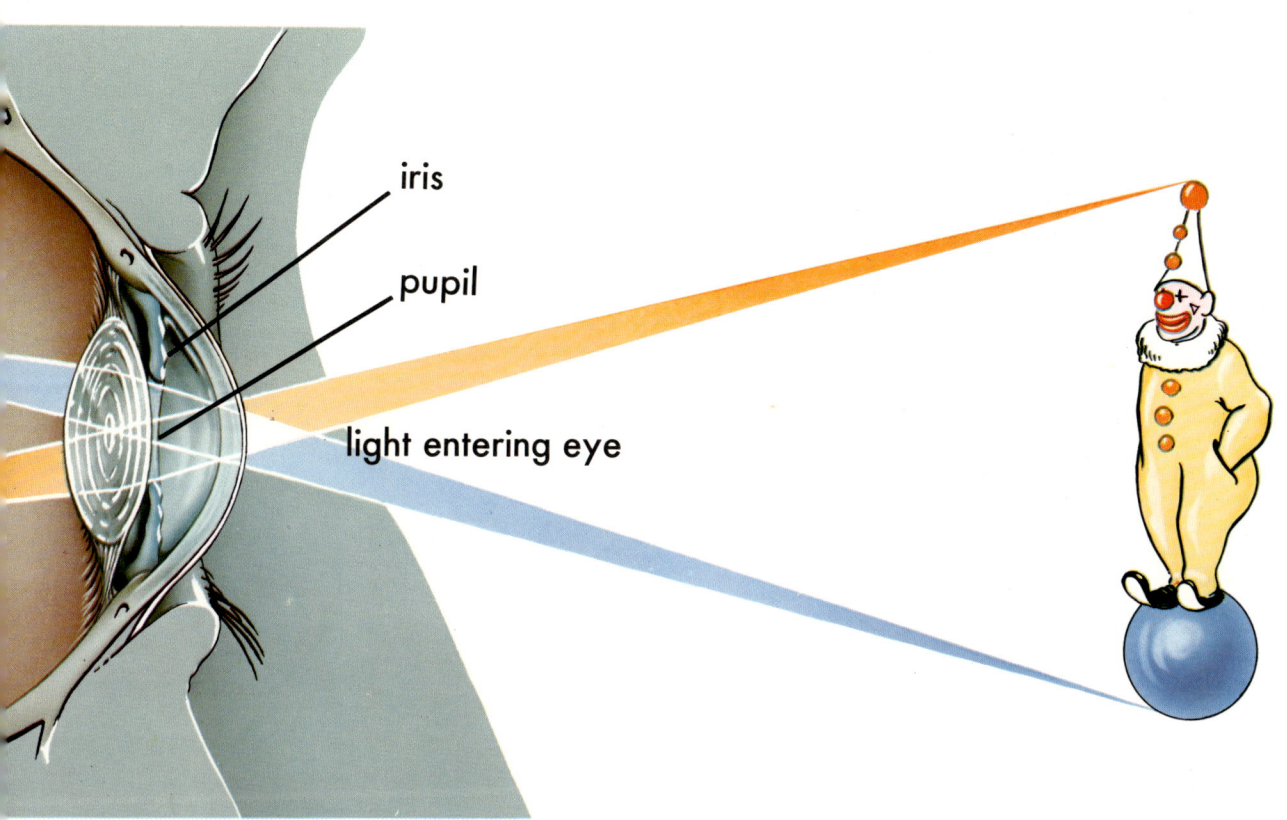

iris

pupil

light entering eye

Light enters your eye through the pupil – the black part in the middle. In bright light, your pupil is small. Only a little light can enter your eye.

Long John Silver is lifting the patch from his eye. The pupil is large because the eye has been in the dark. The pupil in his other eye is much smaller because it has been in the daylight.

Tricks your eyes play on you

Look at the top picture. Now move your eyes closer to it, until your nose is resting on the page. It looks as if the whale has swallowed the fisherman.

Now look at the black oblongs. After a while you will see grey blobs beginning to form in the white spaces.

Some people are 'colour-blind'. This means they cannot tell the difference between some colours. Can you see the number hidden in this circle?

In the picture below, is the blue line the same length as the red line? Measure the two lines.

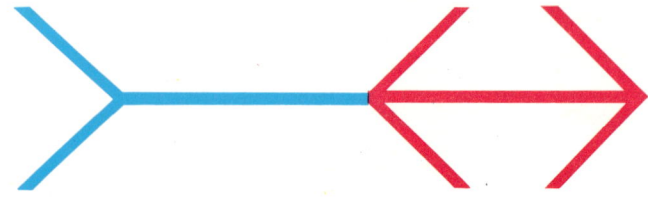

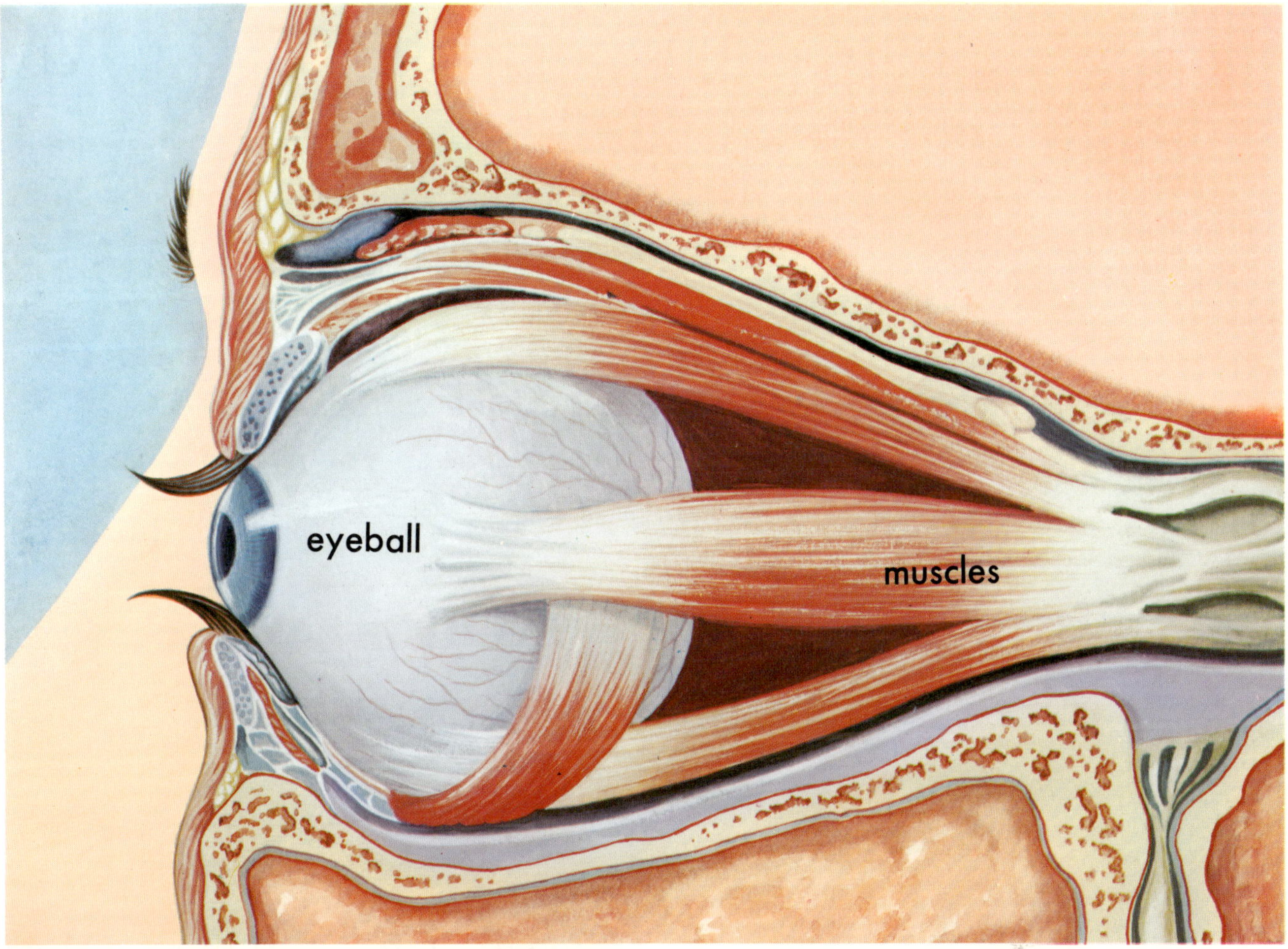

eyeball

muscles

This is a picture of your eye inside your head. You can see how like a ball it is.

You can move your eyes to left and right, up and down or round in a circle. This is because you have six muscles attached to each eye.
This astronaut is looking sideways. Notice that both his eyes are looking the same way.
You cannot move one eye without the other.

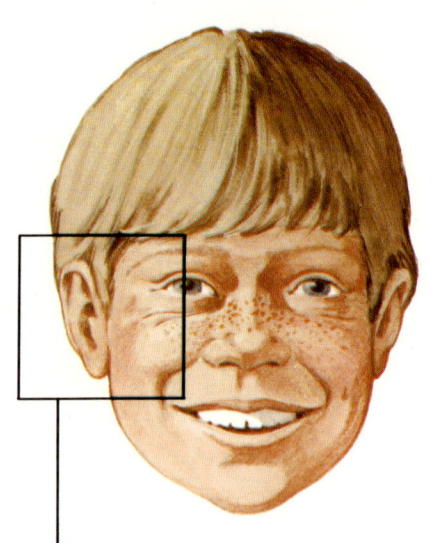

Hearing

The most important parts of your ears are inside your head. Sounds are very tiny, fast movements in the air. They are called vibrations. Vibrations pass along a tube to your eardrum and make your eardrum vibrate. Nerve messages about the vibrations go to your brain and so you hear a sound.

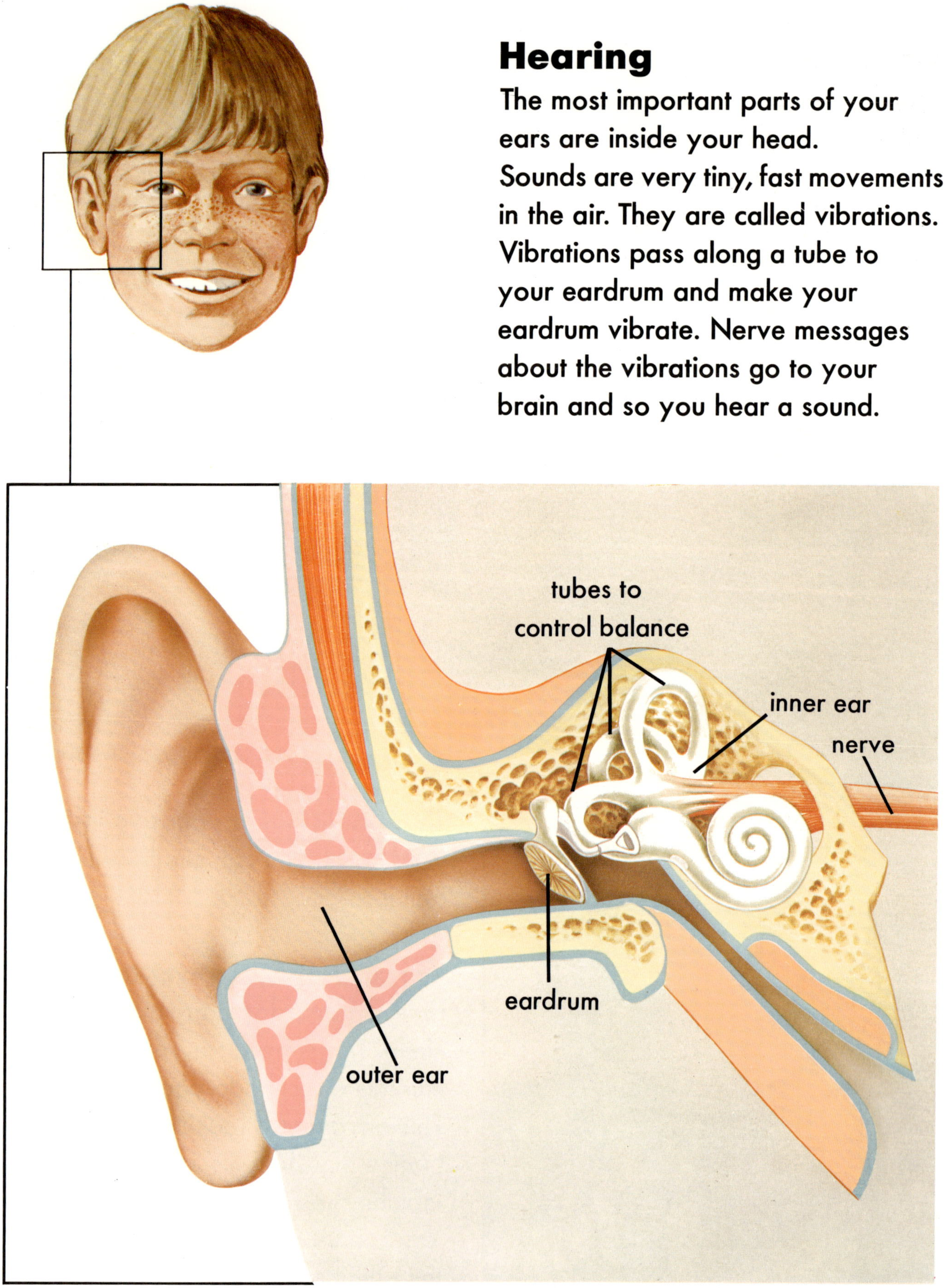

tubes to
control balance

inner ear

nerve

eardrum

outer ear

Balance

This boy is using his sense of balance to help him ride his bicycle. Tiny tubes in your ears control balance. If you feel dizzy it means that your balance has probably been upset for some reason.

Your body has a sense of its own size and position. Shut your eyes and try touching the end of your nose with your finger.

Taste and smell

There are four basic different tastes — sweet, sour, salty and bitter. Different parts of your tongue can taste each one.

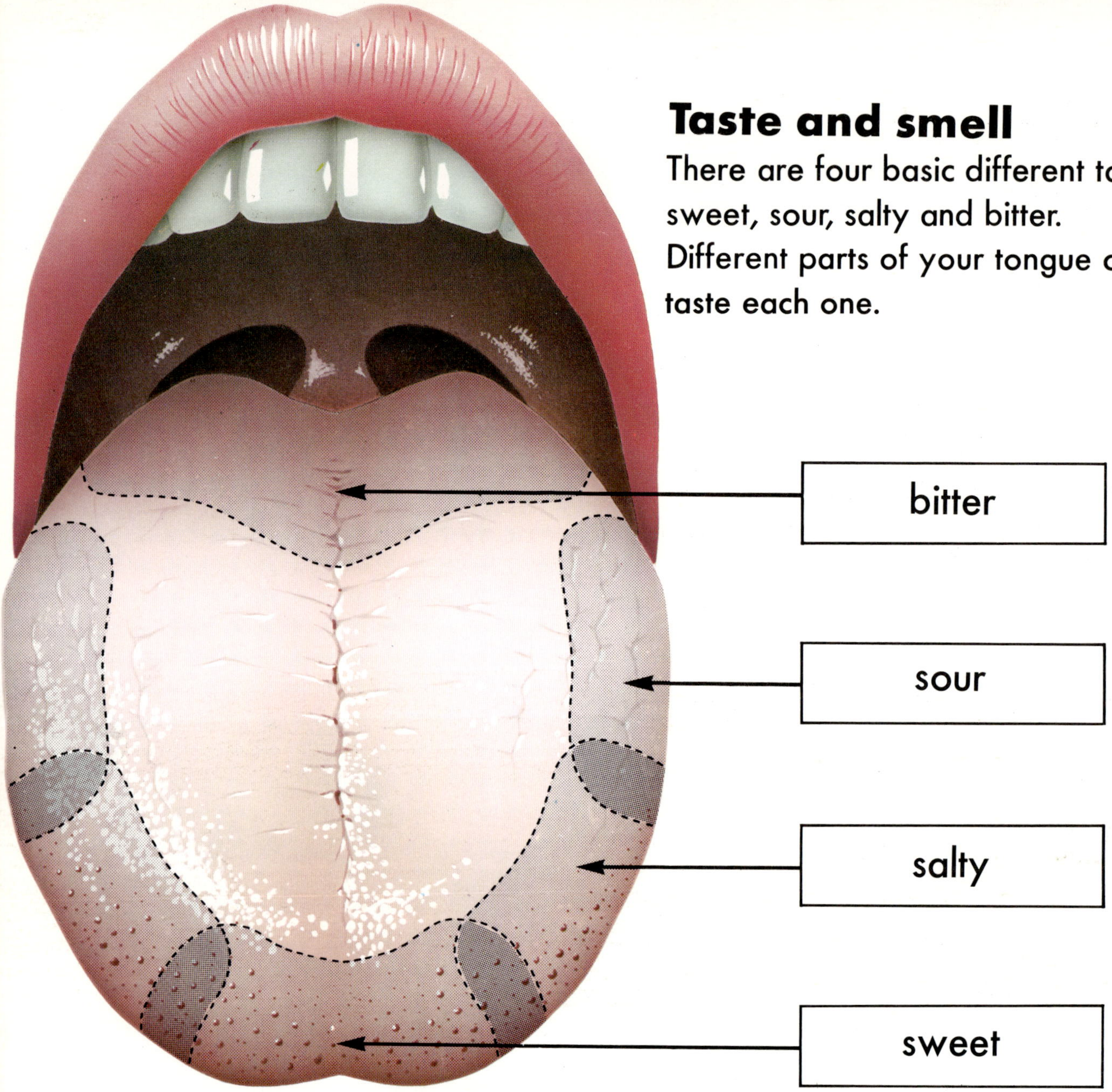

bitter

sour

salty

sweet

The little bumps on your tongue are taste buds. Try testing your taste areas. Put a little sugar on the tip of your tongue. It will taste sweet. Now notice the difference if you put some sugar right at the back of your tongue.

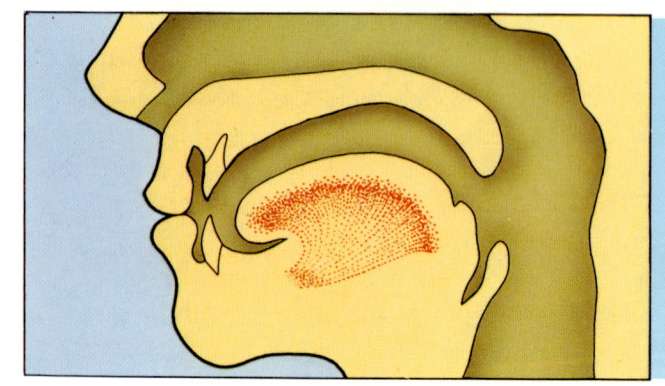

40

There are many different kinds of smell, however. Nerves inside your nose make you notice them all. The mouth and nose openings join up at the back of your throat.

Try tasting different kinds of food with your eyes shut. Guess what they are. Now do it holding your nose. It is much more difficult to guess. You have to smell food as well as tasting it to enjoy its real 'flavour'.

Touch

Your skin can only feel five different sensations. You can see them in the picture.

First of all, there is a feeling of pressure. Next there is a feeling of pain when you hurt yourself.

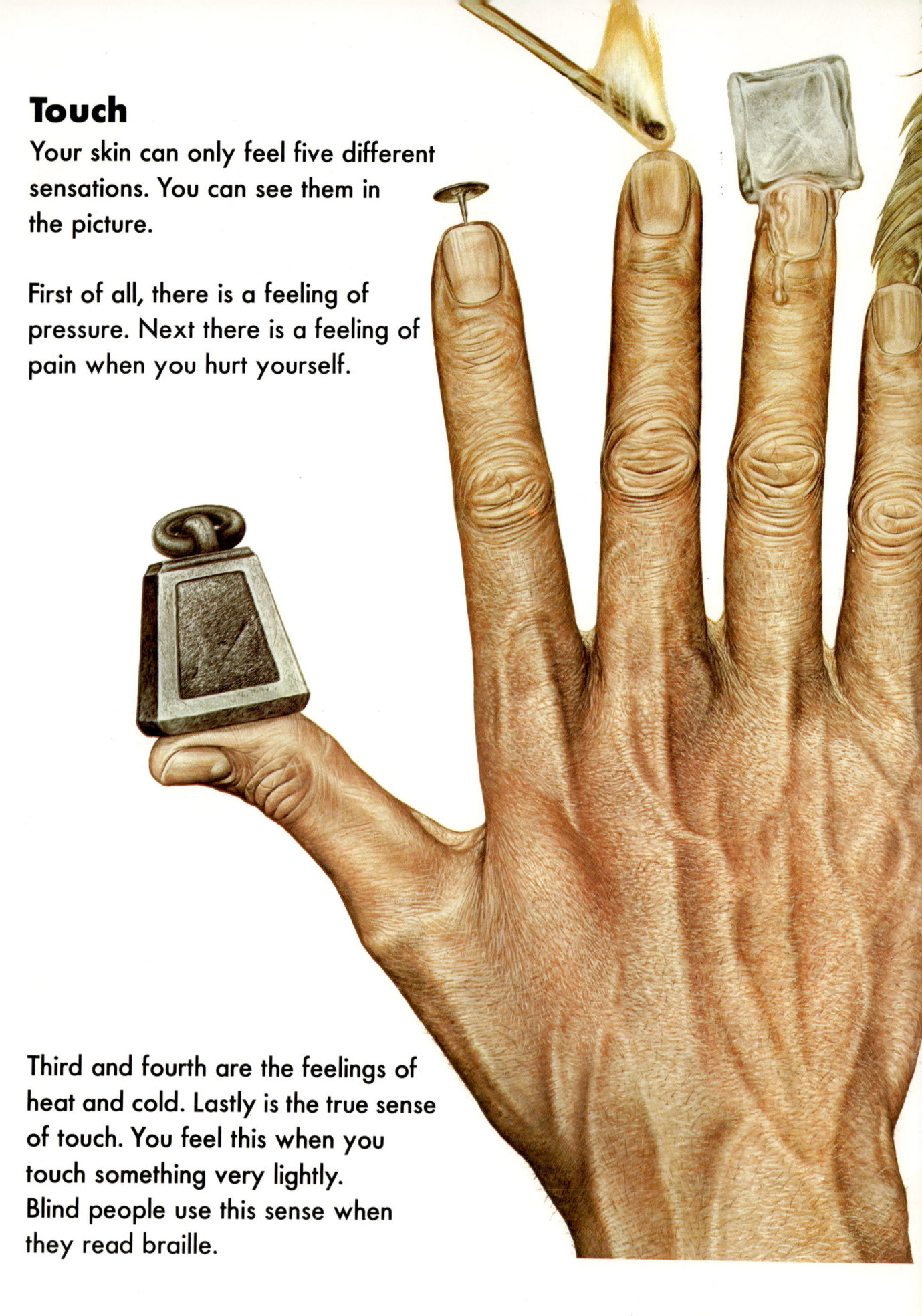

Third and fourth are the feelings of heat and cold. Lastly is the true sense of touch. You feel this when you touch something very lightly. Blind people use this sense when they read braille.

If a crab pinches your toe, your foot jerks away from the pain very quickly. A nerve message from your toe does not have to go as far as your brain before you move your foot. It takes a short cut. It only goes as far as your backbone. This kind of quick movement is called a reflex action.

Books for blind people use a special writing called braille. The letters are made of patterns of little dots that stick up above the surface of the paper.

Do you know why?

People yawn when they are tired. They shiver when they are cold and sweat when they are hot. Sometimes when you get the hiccups you cannot stop. All these are things which you cannot control. Your body does them to keep itself healthy. On these pages you can see why some of these things happen.

When something gets into your nose, you sneeze. The blast of air pushes out anything that is irritating the inside of your nose.

Sometimes you blush when you feel embarrassed. The tiny blood vessels in your face get bigger. This allows extra blood to flow into them, and makes your face turn red. No-one knows why people blush.

People often yawn when they feel tired. Yawning makes you take in a deep breath of air. When you do this your body takes in more oxygen. This helps your body to feel less tired.

Whether it is hot or cold outside, your body always stays at the same temperature. When you feel cold, your muscles start to shiver. They are trying to make heat to keep you warm.

When it is cold, the hairs on your skin stand up in goose pimples. Once, people had more hair on their bodies and this trapped the air and helped to keep them warm.

Your body can keep itself cool as well as warm. In hot weather, sweat glands send water up to the surface of the skin. The water evaporates and takes away some of the body's heat.

WHAT HAPPENS WHEN YOU ARE ILL?

If you are ill, you must go to bed and rest so that your body can work at getting better. In a hospital, doctors and nurses look after you. They find out exactly what is wrong with you.

A doctor is listening to one boy's chest to check his heartbeat. Another boy has had an accident. He has hurt his head and broken his arm.

This boy is covered with spots. He is in a separate room because he has measles. Other children might catch it if he stayed in the same ward.

Breaks, burns and cuts

If you fall down hard, you may break a bone. Never move anyone who may have a broken bone.

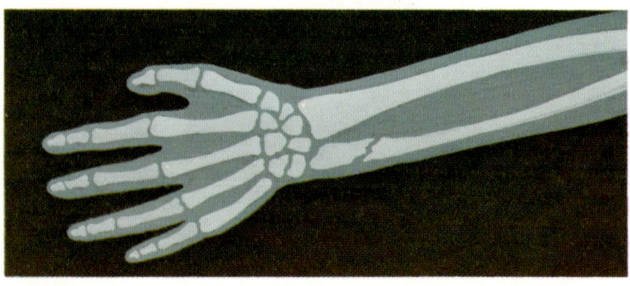

The doctor takes an X-ray photograph of the broken bone. It shows him where the break is.

Plaster put round the arm hardens. It keeps the broken ends still. The ends grow together again.

A burn can hurt quite a lot. This boy should put his arm under the cold water tap straightaway to make the burn less.

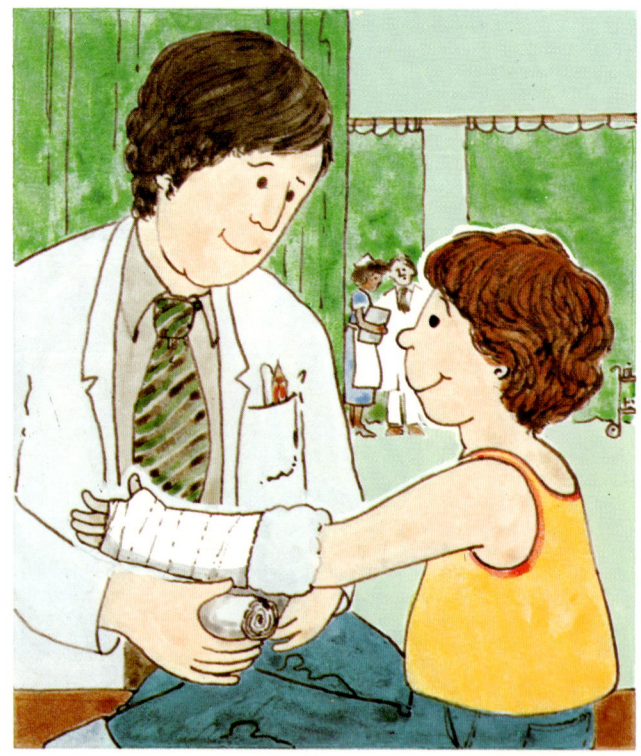

If a burn is bad, you must see a doctor. He may put on a bandage to keep out dirt and germs.

If a cut bleeds a lot, call an adult. Press a clean handkerchief on to stop it bleeding.

Nosebleeds are quite common. They can be caused by a bump on the nose, or by blowing your nose too hard.

This girl's mother is washing her grazed knee with water to clean it. A plaster keeps out dirt.

If you have a nosebleed, sit with your head over a bowl or a sink. Pinch your nostrils together. Put a cold, wet handkerchief over your nose for ten minutes.

Fighting disease

Germs getting into your body make you ill. Your body can learn to fight off germs. Doctors help it do this by giving you very tiny doses of the germs. Next time you come into contact with a big dose of those germs, your body knows how to fight them off. This process is called immunization.

Different germs carry different diseases. The liquid on this sugar lump immunizes against polio.

Joseph Lister found out that germs grow best in dirt. Today hospitals and operating theatres are kept very clean so that there are as few germs around as possible. This helps stop disease spreading.

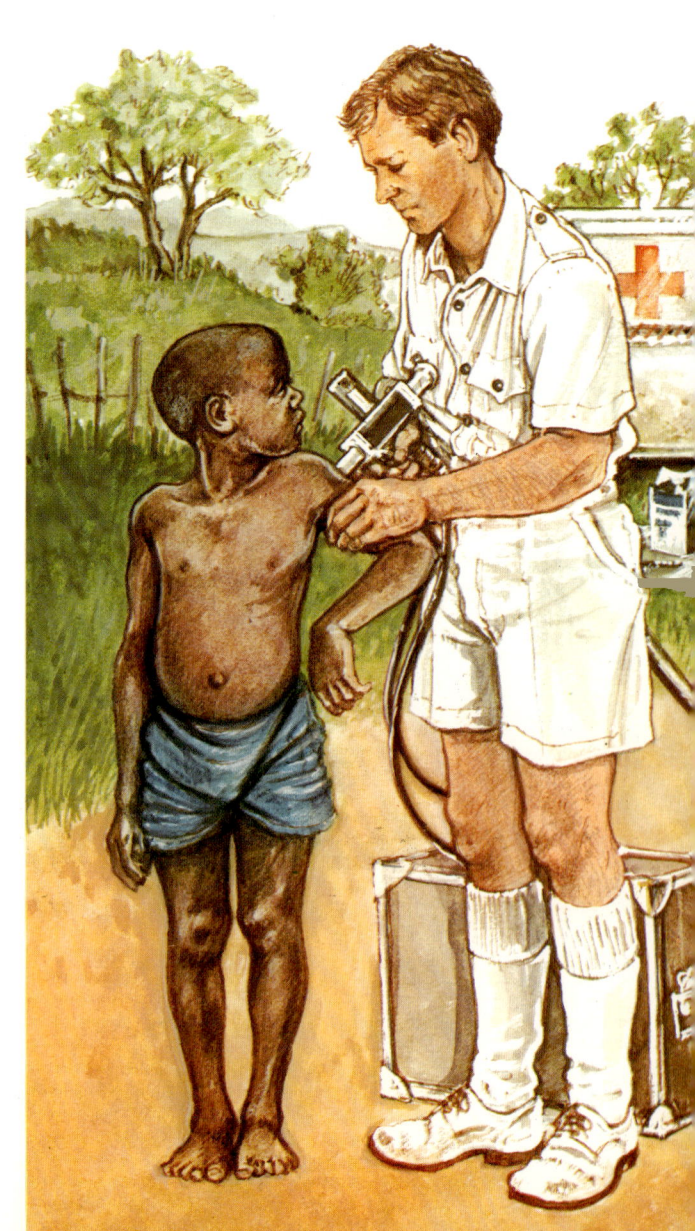

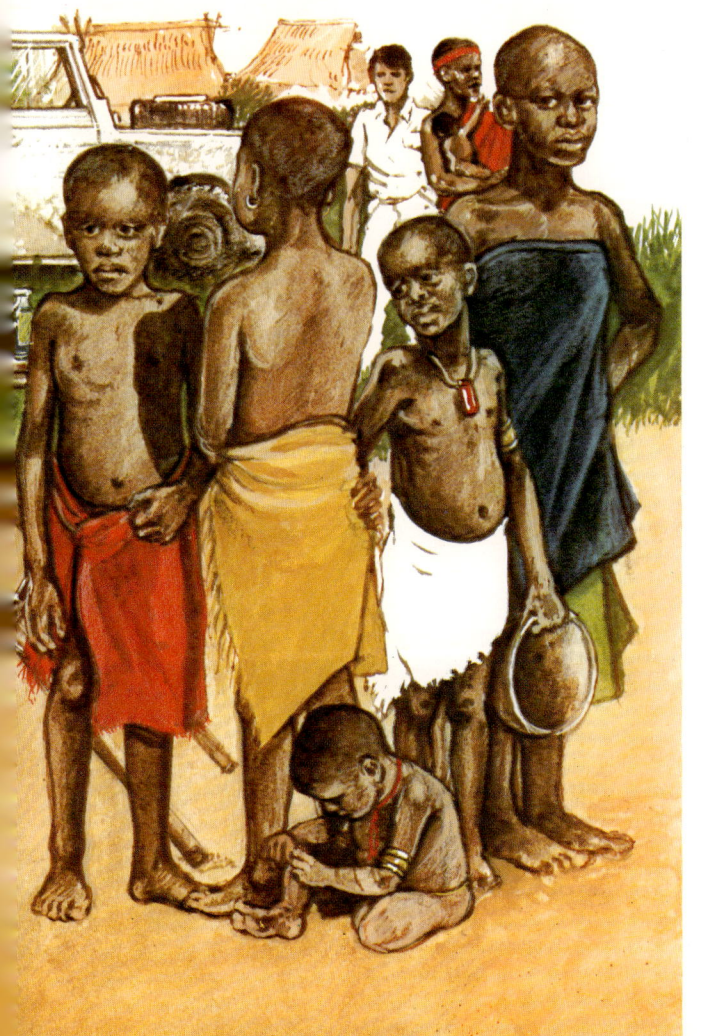

Immunization only protects you against some diseases. If you do become ill, your body is very good at fighting off disease. Scientists have discovered chemicals that help your body kill germs. These chemicals are made into pills and medicines.

When you went to see your doctor to be immunized, he probably used a 'syringe' to give you an injection. Doctors can immunize large numbers of people very quickly. This doctor on the left is using a special immunization gun to immunize some African children.

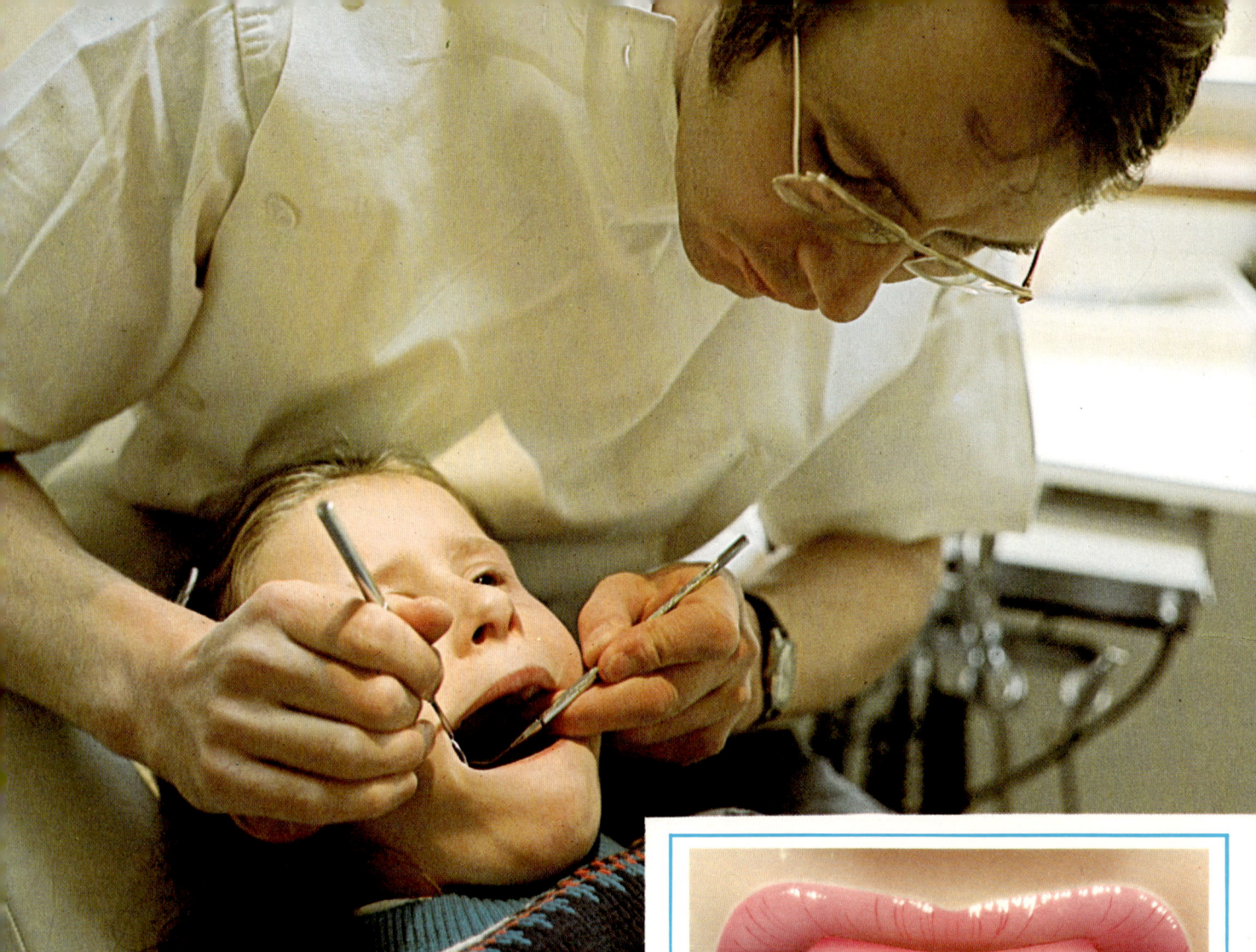

Keeping Healthy

Tooth decay is caused by germs rotting away the hard enamel that covers your teeth. Decay may give you toothache.

You should go to see the dentist regularly. If he sees any tooth decay he will fill the decayed tooth with special cement. This stops the decay getting worse.

Germs grow on bits of food left in-between your teeth. Get rid of these bits by brushing your teeth after meals and before you go to bed at night.

Germs can get on to food from dirty hands. Then the germs get into your body and can make you ill. Do not forget to wash your hands after going to the toilet and before meals.

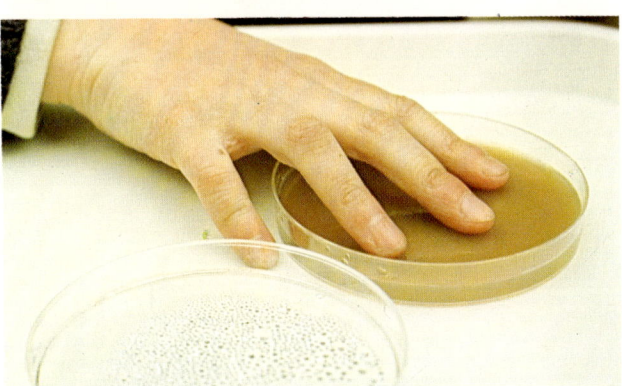

Germs live all around us. The germs from a dirty hand have been specially grown in this dish. The dark patches which you can see contain millions of tiny germs.

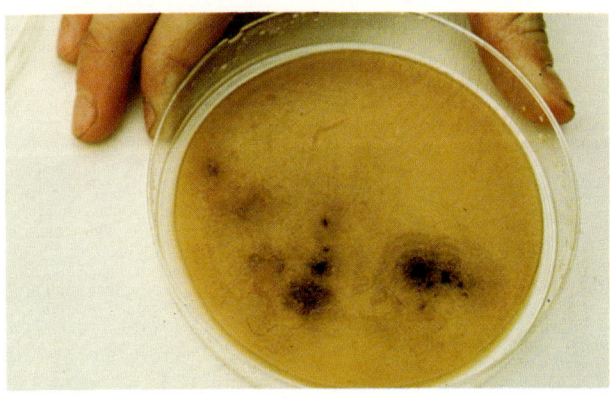

Going to the Doctor

Most people feel ill sometimes. It is the doctor's job to find out what is wrong with them. Patients usually go to see the doctor at his surgery. He can treat most illnesses there.

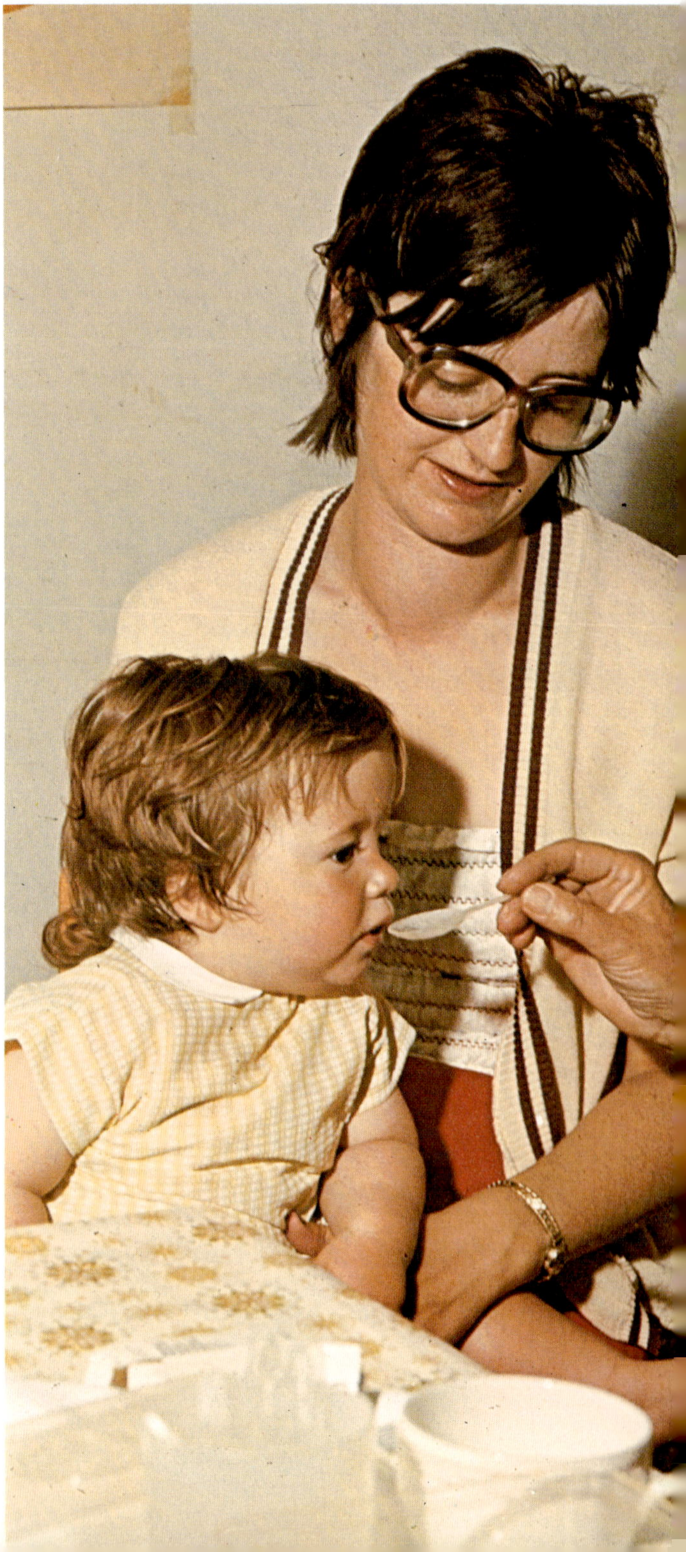

Medicines help your body get better when you are not feeling well.
This boy has a sore throat and a headache. He has tonsilitis. The spoonful of medicine in his tummy passes into his blood. It travels all round his body in his blood. Gradually, it kills the germs that cause tonsilitis.

Some illnesses need special care. Then, it is best to go into hospital. This child is taking some medicine at the doctor's surgery. The medicine will immunize the child against polio.

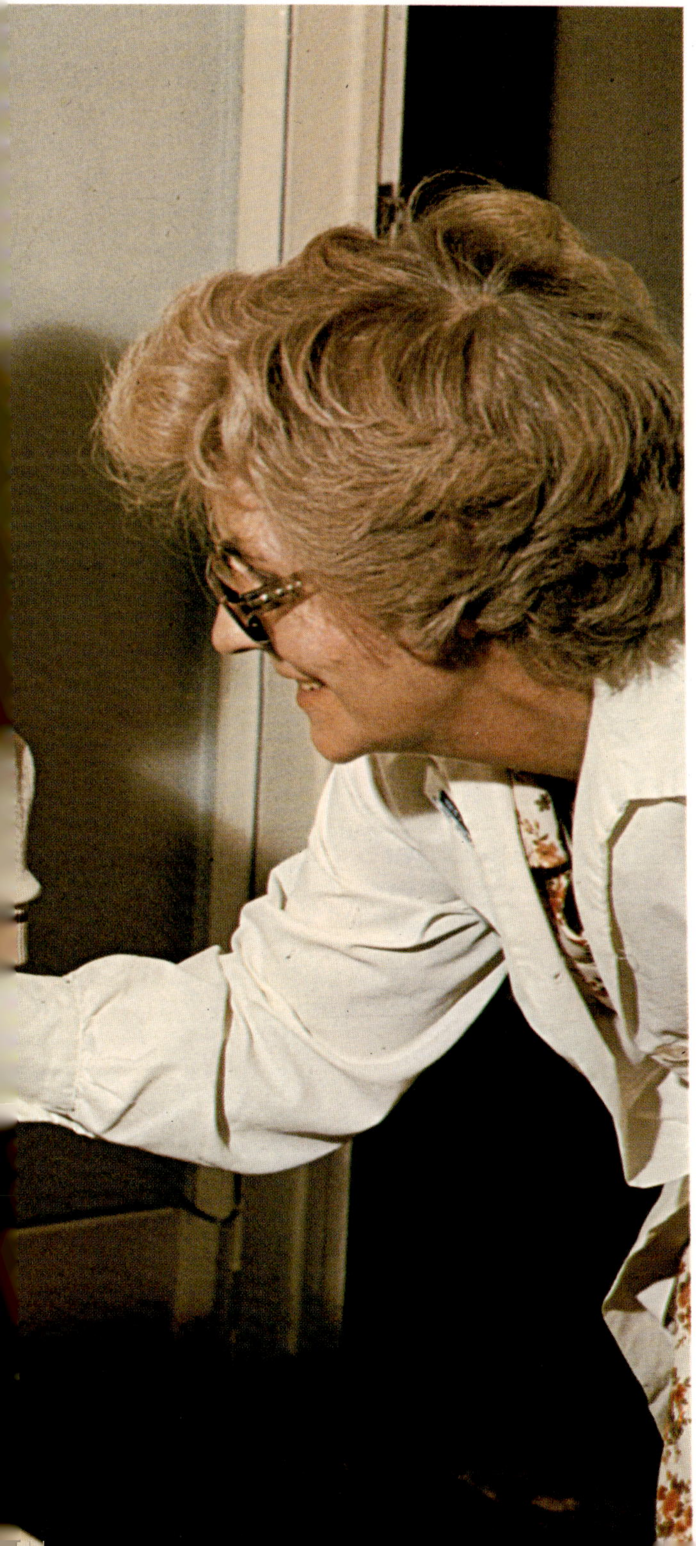

When you visit the doctor he will probably want to examine you. That is why you might have to take off your clothes. He will listen to your chest with a tube called a stethoscope. He will have a good look down your throat and into your ears. Once he knows what is wrong, the doctor can decide what medicine will help you.

You can get your medicine at the chemist's. The doctor writes an instruction to the chemist called a prescription. It tells the chemist what it is you need. Medicines are useful. They are also very powerful. If you take too much all at once they can be dangerous. Never play with medicines. Only take them when a grown-up gives them to you.

Discoveries about the body

At one time, people did not know why they became ill. They tried to cure diseases with magic. No-one had ever studied the inside of the human body. Later, some people began to find out how the body works. They discovered what goes wrong and why. Today doctors can cure people of many illnesses.

William Harvey discovered that the heart pumps blood around the body. Here he is explaining his ideas.

X-rays take photographs of bones and organs. They were discovered by Wilhelm Rontgen. He took the first X-ray of his wife's hand.

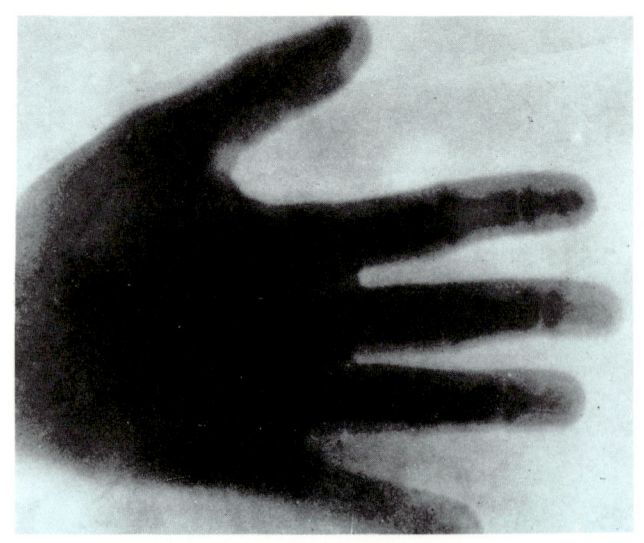

Your body is made up of millions of cells. These cells are very tiny. You need a microscope to see them. Anton van Leeuwenhoek made the first microscope.

Morton

Before you have an operation, a doctor gives you an anaesthetic. This stops you feeling any pain. William Morton used ether, a kind of anaesthetic, over 100 years ago.

Rene Laènnec invented the stethoscope. He got the idea from listening to a patient's heart through a rolled-up piece of paper.

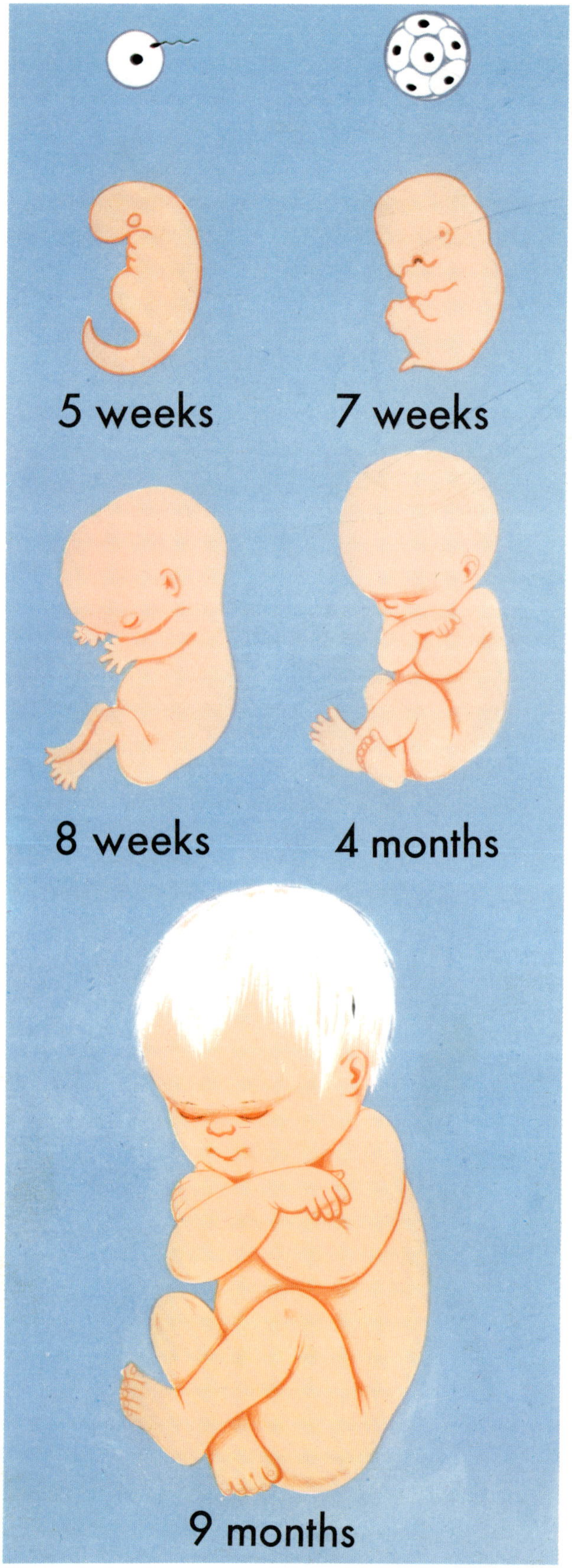

Growing up

A baby begins life as an egg in its mother's womb. At first it is as small as a full stop. Two months later, the baby's shape is already formed. The mother's body protects the baby while it is growing.

5 weeks

7 weeks

8 weeks

4 months

9 months

This woman is going to have a baby. She is pregnant. As her baby grows larger, her tummy gets more rounded to make room for it. After six months, she can feel her baby move inside her. After nine months, the baby is ready to be born.

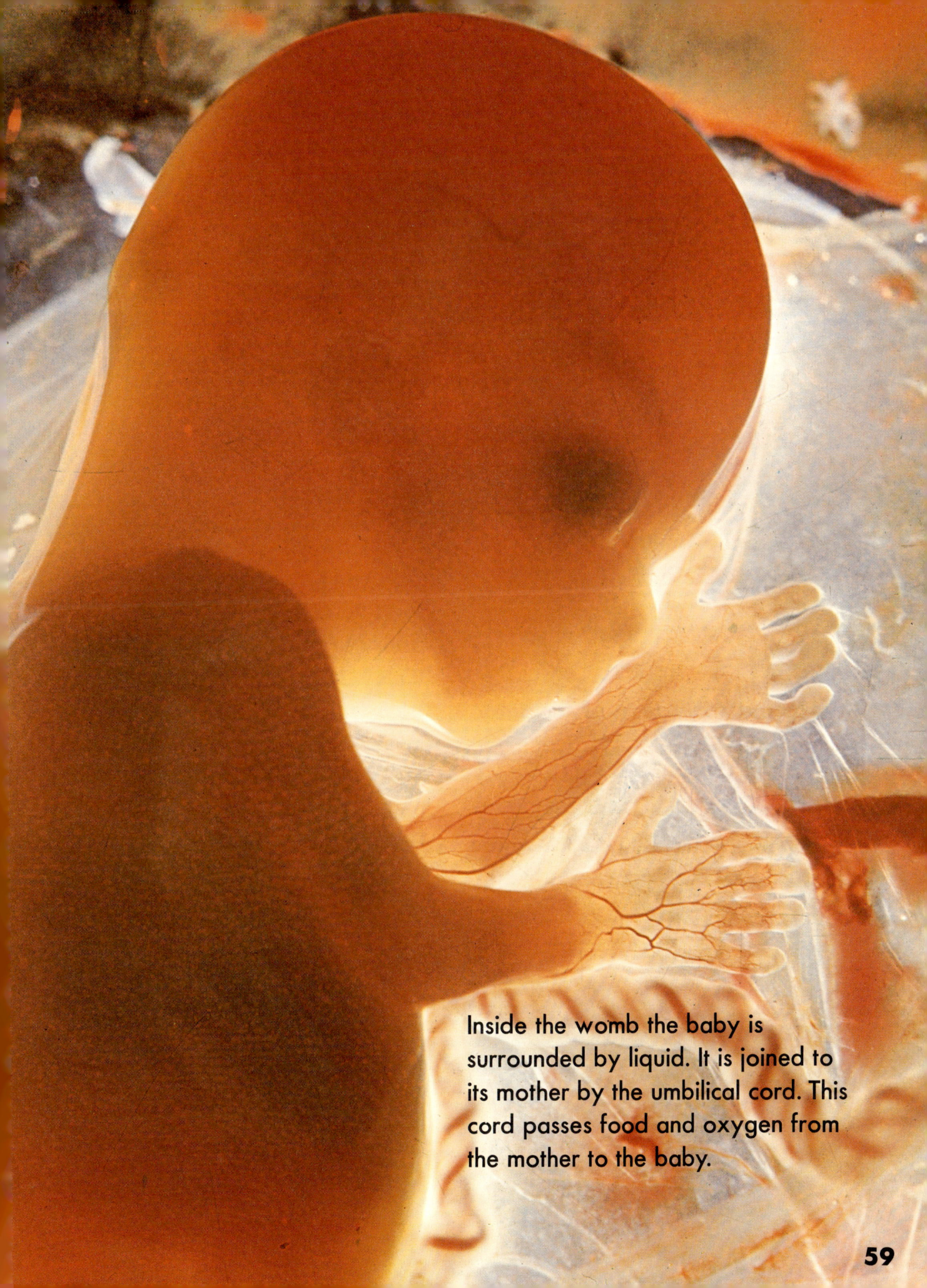

Inside the womb the baby is surrounded by liquid. It is joined to its mother by the umbilical cord. This cord passes food and oxygen from the mother to the baby.

The birth of a baby

Mothers usually go into hospital to have their babies. Doctors and nurses help each mother to have her baby.

Mother and the new baby will stay in hospital for a few days. When they are both healthy and strong they can go home.

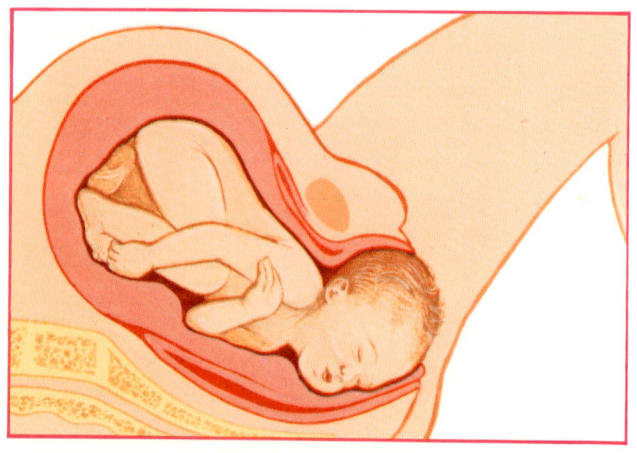

The mother's muscles push the baby out through her vagina between her legs. The umbilical cord still joins the mother to her baby. This cord has to be cut. Your navel is the place where the cord was once attached to you.

A young baby cannot eat the kind of food you eat for quite a while. It does not have teeth when it is born. It may drink milk from its mother's breasts. It may have special milk from a bottle fitted with a teat, like the baby in this picture. Perhaps you have a young brother or sister at home the same age as this little baby.

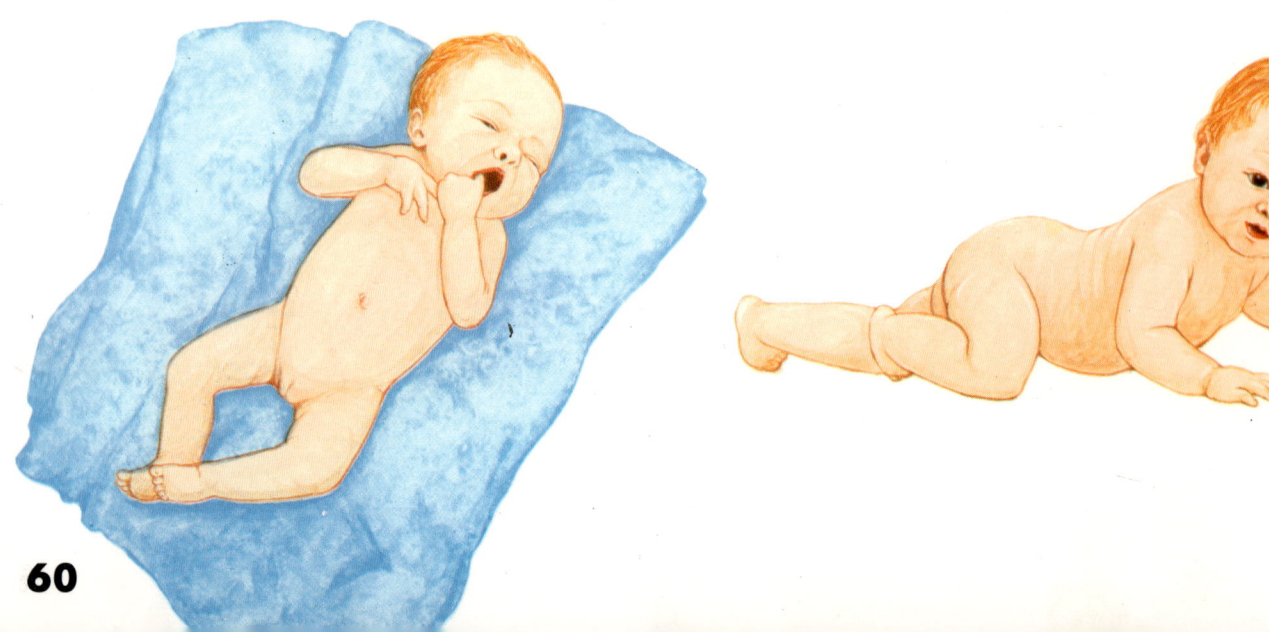

A young baby has to be carefully looked after. It cannot walk or talk or do anything for itself. But babies do cry to let people know when they are hungry or cold or tired.

Babies grow very quickly. First they learn to sit up by themselves. Between 10 and 18 months most of them take their first steps. Then they start to say their first words.

How long do we live?

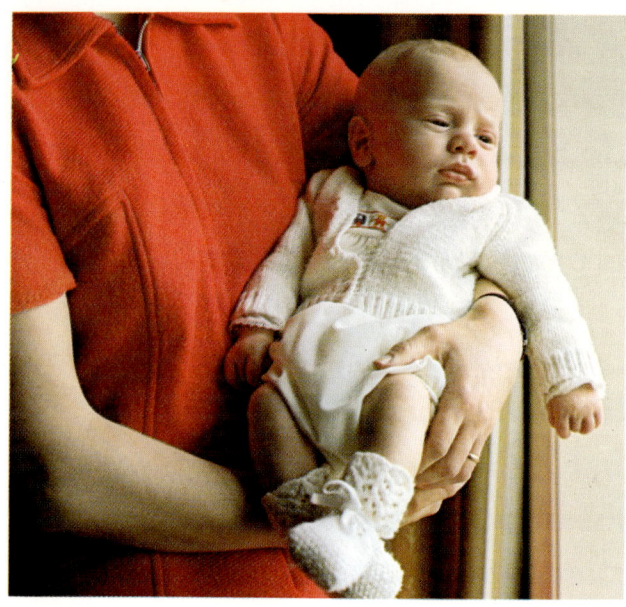

People change a lot in appearance as they get older. This baby is only a few months old.

The boy in this picture is seven years old. Perhaps he is about the same age as you.

Pelican

Elephant

Parrot

Man

Rat

Hippopotamus

Sheep

Cat

Seal

Dog

Frog

Here is a boy with his father. The boy is 13. His father is about three times his age.

This cheerful old lady is 76 years old. There are a lot of people who live to be even older than this.

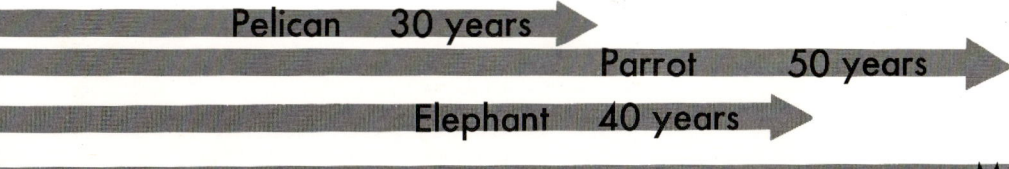

Pelican   30 years

Parrot   50 years

Elephant   40 years

Man   70 years

Rat   3 years

Hippopotamus   40 years

Sheep   10 years

Seal   15 years

Dog   13 years

Cat   13 years

Frog   5 years

Many people live for 70 or even 80 years. Few people live to be over 100. Most animals live for a much shorter time. A few animals live for as long as 40 or 50 years. They include some elephants, hippopotami and some parrots.

DID YOU KNOW?

You have 206 bones in your body. The smallest is a little bone in your ear. The biggest is your thigh bone.

The strongest men in the world can carry weights of nearly 3 tonnes on their backs. That is even heavier than a Rolls-Royce car!

Our eyesight seems good to us, but a barn owl can see 100 times more sharply than we can.

If you never cut your hair, it would grow to about your waist. One man, an Indian monk, grew his hair until it was nearly 8 metres long.

A man's beard could grow until it reached the ground. The longest beard that a man ever grew was 5½ metres long.

Some people can shout so loudly that they can drown a road drill going full blast.

INDEX

A WAYWARD GENIUS

Neville Northy Burnard

CORNISH SCULPTOR
1818 - 1878

MARY MARTIN

Lodenek Press